RUSSIA

RUSSIA

BY KIM BROWN FADER

LUCENT BOOKS
P.O. BOX 289011
SAN DIEGO, CA 92198-9011

78 936 72

TITLES IN THE MODERN NATIONS SERIES INCLUDE:

Canada
England
Russia

Library of Congress Cataloging-in-Publication Data

Fader, Kim Brown, 1956–
    Russia / by Kim Brown Fader.
        p. cm. — (Modern nations of the world)
    Includes bibliographical references and index.
    Summary: Examines the history of the country now known as the Russian Federation, from its earliest days through its role as part of the Soviet Union to its current place in the world.
    ISBN 1-56006-521-4 (alk. paper)
    1. Russia—History—Juvenile literature. 2. Soviet Union—History—Juvenile literature. 3. Russia (Federation)—History—Juvenile literature. [1. Russia—History. 2. Soviet Union—History. 3. Russia (Federation)—History.] I. Title. II. Series.
  DK41.F33 1998
  947—dc21   97-29557
                                                                                                     CIP
                                                                                                      AC

Copyright © 1998 by Lucent Books, Inc.
P.O. Box 289011, San Diego, CA 92198-9011
Printed in the U.S.A.

CONTENTS

INTRODUCTION

UNDERSTANDING RUSSIA

It is not at all easy to describe a country as vast as the Russian Federation. Sprawling across eastern Europe and northern Asia, its size challenges the imagination. When the sun is setting in Kaliningrad, the small, separated kernel of Russia wedged between Poland and Lithuania, on the coast of the Baltic Sea, it is rising the following day in Vladivostok, the terminal point of the Trans-Siberian railroad on the Sea of Japan. From Moscow, Russia's capital city, to any of its borders is at least a full day's drive. Consider this astounding comparison: The geographic region known as Siberia, stretching from the Ural Mountains to the Pacific coast, is an area larger than the lit surface of the moon.

Russia's immense expanse is hardly disturbed by natural obstacles. The Ural Mountains, with elevations only occasionally rising above three thousand feet were easy to scale. The vast level plains known as the Russian steppe were crossed in all directions by great surges of people. As Russia west of the Urals developed into a nation, colonizing the territories to the east and south became its greatest task, an expansion similar in some ways to the settling of the American frontier.

A UNIQUE AND COMPLICATED HISTORY

Both Asian and European, Russia has many basic connections to European history and culture. However, Russia's history differs from Europe's in important ways. Russia was never part of the Roman Empire, and never experienced the transmission of culture from ancient times that shaped western European nations. Europe was never conquered by the Mongol warriors, whose tight grip on Russia for over two centuries meant that Russia was isolated from the tremendous scientific and cultural leap forward of the Renaissance. In the years England produced Queen Elizabeth I and Shakespeare's great plays, Russia was suffering under the tyranni-

cal, ultimately ruinous rule of Ivan the Terrible. Peter the Great was the first Russian ruler with aspirations to Westernize and modernize his country, and his landmark reforms began a new era. Nevertheless, throughout the eighteenth and nineteenth centuries Russia was largely undeveloped, the overwhelming majority of its people uneducated, all serving an autocrat in a system with little regard or opportunity for individual initiative.

A typical scene from eighteenth-century Russia shows Cathedral Place in Moscow. Throughout the eighteenth and nineteenth centuries, Russia remained backward compared to advances being made elsewhere.

The twentieth century saw a radical transformation of the Russian state, which rapidly became a counterweight to the United States as a world power. However, despite the technological and economic achievements and utopian promise of a better life for all under communist rule, the Soviet system proved only too similar to earlier despotic regimes. That so great an empire as the Union of Soviet Socialist Republics (USSR) gave way with so little loss of life is certainly one of the most amazing developments of modern times.

The new Russian Federation faces new challenges. Arms control, the safeguarding of nuclear materials, and the development of legal and economic institutions to support Russia's reorganized society and economy are some of the important issues that will accompany this nation into the twenty-first century.

1

THE FIRST RUSSIA: LAND OF THE SLAVIC PEOPLE

There is a wide stretch of terrain in Russia, from the Black Sea to southeastern Siberia, where the soil is loose, crumbly, and a deep black color; it is rich in humus in a layer more than two feet deep, deeper than a plow can furrow. Although the winters are severe and the summers short and sometimes given to drought, for eons grain has been grown there. If the earliest groups of settled people who inhabited this "black earth" region had been left alone, the history of Russia would have been entirely different. But the indigenous farming people had no natural barriers to protect them. Hardy warrior tribes of nomadic people, many from the heart of Asia, swept across the steppe, or prairie, ready to claim the infinite, fertile pastures as their own.

EARLY NOMADIC CULTURES

The Scythians, a people almost constantly on the move with their herds of horses and cattle, ruled a vast area arcing north of the Black Sea from the Danube River to the Caucasus Mountains from about 800 to 200 B.C. Their rule was one in a long series of nomadic empires, each eclipsed by the forceful entry of dominant newcomers.

An Indo-European people migrating from the Asiatic steppe and speaking an Iranian language, the Scythians were divided into many tribes called hordes, subject to the authority of the king of the main horde. The fifth-century B.C. Greek historian Herodotus came in contact with them in his travels and was impressed by the advantage they had over their enemies: "Having neither cities, nor forts, and carrying their dwellings with them wherever they go; accustomed, moreover, one and all of them, to shoot from horseback; and living not by husbandry [farming] but on their cattle, their wagons the only houses that they possess, how can they fail of being unconquerable, and unassailable even?"[1] They used saddles (which neither the Greeks nor the Romans had) and ate mare's milk and boiled meat. Fierce in battle and brutally vengeful, they were known for scalping their opponents and brandishing human skulls and skins.

Despite their savagery and nomadic lifestyle, the Scythians also had an appreciation of the fine goods of civilization. Remarkable caches of Scythian belongings, such as jewelry, weapons, cups, and bowls, made from or adorned with gold or silver, have been recovered from their kurgans, or burial mounds. Some kurgans rise to a height of sixty-five feet, marking the passage of these people across the steppe. Their treasures reveal a wide range of contact with other cultures, especially the Greeks, who had established colonies on the north shore of the Black Sea. Some historians believe that the foundations of Russian folk art, with the common subjects of bull, deer, goat , bear, and bird, reach back to this period.

By the middle of the second century B.C. the Scythian Empire had broken down, yielding to a tribe known as the Sarmatians. Like the Scythians, the Sarmatians emerged from Asia and spoke an Iranian language. They held sway on the steppe until approximately A.D. 200. Sarmatian chieftains accumulated great wealth and fostered the commercial contacts between the steppe people and the Greek (and later, Roman) colonies on the Black Sea. Their heavy armor, wall paintings, and jewel-encrusted enamel and gold ornaments have also been found in burial sites in the Crimea, the peninsula of Ukraine splitting the Sea of Azov from the Black Sea.

THE SLAVS

A new tribal name appears in the historical record during the period of Sarmatian rule. Roman historians Pliny and Tacitus call them the Venedi; the Germans called them the Wend. The Venedi, remarked Tacitus in his famous book on Germany written in A.D. 98, "have fixed abodes, carry shields, and delight to use their feet . . . all of which traits are opposite to those of the Sarmatians, who live in wagons and on horseback."[2] The names of related tribes mentioned by the Gothic historian Jordanis, writing in the sixth century, include the Sclaveni, the Antes, and the Spali. It is now

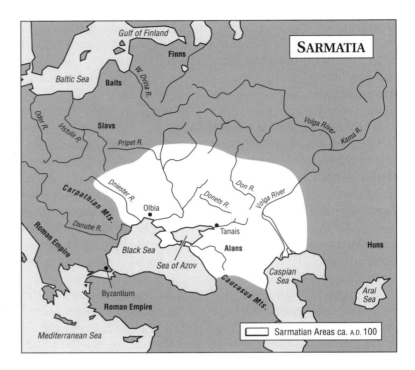

accepted that these were names of Slavic tribes. Single Slavic tribes and clans were known under various other names, many of which remain unknown.

The Slavs originally lived northeast of the Carpathian Mountains, near rivers such as the Vistula (in present-day Poland), the Pripet (in southern Belarus and Ukraine), the upper Dniester (in Ukraine), and the Don (in Russia). The oldest place names in this area are exclusively Slavic; beyond this area, the oldest names are derived from a mixture of languages.

Information about the ancient Slavs is scarce and uncertain, drawn primarily from linguistic sources and archaeological digs. They were neither racially nor politically united, but did speak a common language. They gradually spread northward, into the lands of the Lithuanians and Finns, and to the southeast, from the Baltic to the Black Sea. But in these ancient times they were a mere fraction of the tumultuous whole.

ETHNIC UPHEAVALS

Great waves of warring, migrating peoples were crossing the steppe in the area of modern-day southern Russia, Belarus, and Ukraine. Each, for a time, took control over steppe dwellers like the Slavs. In A.D. 200 the Goths, Germanic tribes from the Baltic Sea region, marched to the Black Sea, defeating the Sarmatians and destroying the Roman colonies on the north shore of the Black Sea. By 400 they had subdued most Slavic tribes.

By the middle of the fifth century, however, the Goths were driven westward by the fleet and menacing Huns, a heavily armed nomadic group migrating across the steppe, dislocated by ethnic upheavals in middle Eurasia. As of the year 450 the Huns dominated the area between the Volga and Rhine Rivers, and then, under their leader, Attila, pushed south into France and Italy. Most Slavs fell under Hun domination. But the empire of the Huns quickly fell apart, and the Germanic tribes crossed into Britain and France. The Slavs were then free to spread their settlements to the Elbe and Danube Rivers and throughout Germany. Eventually, these western migrating Slavic groups became known as the Poles, the Czechs, and the Slovaks. Continuing pressure from the Avars, another conquering Asiatic tribe, pushed the southern

THE STEPPE AND "BLACK EARTH"

The Russian steppe, or prairie, was of paramount importance in shaping the lives of its early inhabitants. Originally covered by tall grasses, the steppe was inhabited both by primitive farmers and by nomadic people who moved with herds of grazing animals. The plumes of grass hid the rich soil beneath, known as the "black earth," or *chernozem* in Russian. This fertile soil was formed by the long accumulation of the decomposition of the grasses. Fine textured and rich in lime, the black earth's fertility is enhanced by abundant earthworms and other soil fauna.

Known not only for its rich soil, the steppe before the plow was a landscape of immense beauty. The nineteenth-century writer Nikolay Gogol, who saw part of the steppe in pristine condition, described it thus: "There could be nothing more beautiful in the world: the visible surface of the earth looked like a golden green ocean, its waves topped by multi-colored spume."

The black earth belt covers about one-fourth of European Russia, an area as large as France, stretching from Romania to the Ural Mountains, and south to the mountains of the Crimea and the Caucasus. Its greatest breadth is in the valley of the Don River, over six hundred miles wide.

Although the Slavs attempted to occupy and cultivate the steppe, they were frequently forced back into the woodlands areas by repeated nomadic invasions.

Slavic tribes into Greece by 550, where they were the hostile neighbors of the Byzantine, or eastern Roman, Empire. By the seventh century Slavic peoples were permanently settled throughout the whole of the Balkan Peninsula, becoming the Serbs, Croats, and Slovenes.

The Slavic tribes known as the Antes, or East Slavs, expanded their territory throughout the northern forests of European Russia by the sixth century, sometimes at the expense of Finnish and Lithuanian people already settled in these areas. The East Slavs are the people who became known as the Russians, Ukrainians, and Belorussians.

Attila, king of the Huns. By 450 most Slavs had fallen under Hun domination. Their empire, however, quickly fell apart.

The early settlements of the East Slavs were sparsely populated, consisting of only a few dozen individuals related by birth or marriage. People lived in pit houses with low walls and roofs rising only a few feet above the ground, mounded over with earth for insulation. By cutting and burning timber, they managed to clear fields to plant enough grain and vegetables for their own basic needs. However, the forest soils were quickly depleted and the settlers would have to move on and repeat the whole laborious process.

THE KHAZAR KINGDOM

Rudimentary trade developed between the peoples of the forest and the peoples of the steppe, although its pattern was often disrupted by conflicts and invasions. For a time, trade was controlled by the Khazars, a Turkic group who had settled on the shores of the Caspian Sea by the sixth century and soon after dominated much of the north slope of the Caucasus Mountains. By 650 they were the rulers of the area north of the Black Sea to the Finnish and Slavic settlements of the upper Volga River. They established their capital, Itil, near the modern Russian city of Astrakhan.

Although the Khazars were originally a horde of horsemen lording over the agricultural tribes, they eventually became more settled and farmed the land surrounding their cities on the steppe. According to a description of Itil, from an Arabian writer, "There were many gardens. It is said that they contained 40,000 vineyards."[3] But the Khazars are best known for taking full advantage of their centrality on the steppe and building a diverse commercial empire. The security of the important rivers and connecting land routes was their main objective. They purchased furs, hides, honey, and wax from the Finns and Slavs; horses raised by the Bulgars, an Asiatic group split off from the Huns; furs brought out of Siberia; the grain, meat, and hides of the steppe; crafts, fabrics, and luxury goods from the Orient and Byzantium. Slaves were also a commodity in the markets of Khazar cities. The Khazars themselves exported only fish and fish glue from the Caspian Sea. They welcomed merchants of all lands and faiths, levying a tax of 10 percent on goods sold. They were known to be tolerant of various religions, although their ruling class converted to Judaism. Arabian sources from the tenth century note that in Khazar lands,

"The Moslems have their mosques, the Christians their churches, and the Jews have their synagogues."[4] Each religious group even had its own judges.

THE RISE OF SLAVIC TOWNS

During the era of Khazar supremacy, the Slavs in the forest and steppe became more numerous than any other people in the area, continuing to mingle with and absorb other ethnic elements. They grew to number 4 to 5 million people, and inhabited an area of about a million square miles, with the river system between the settlements of Novgorod and Kiev at its center. They became prodigious traders, making the most of their highly marketable furs (later described by Marco Polo as "among the best and most valuable in the world") and other forest products. Scores of linked trading centers, many of them fortified towns, were built along the waterways—Novgorod, Polotsk, Smolensk, Chernigov, Kiev, Pereslavl, to name a few. Many of these towns were built around a central stronghold, known as a kremlin, that was cut from the giant forest timber. "It is not hard to imagine the scene on a market day in summer at one of these wooden fortresses perched on a hill," writes historian John Lawrence.

> The men were dressed like traditional Russian peasants in large Turkish trousers with brightly embroidered linen shirts, under a long gown. "Russian boots" were already known, but they were a luxury. The rich wore barbaric jewelry of gold, gilt and amber or perhaps some piece of gorgeous Oriental silk or Byzantine needlework. The crowd went barefoot or wore shoes plaited from bast while the well-to-do wore long Russian boots of leather carefully greased for market day. . . . There would be dancing, and Russian men had already learned to dance squatting on their haunches in the way that is still characteristic of them.[5]

Each part of the long trade route connecting Novgorod and Kiev to the Orient depended on the safety and existence of every other. But the individual routes were vulnerable to attack by an endless number of competing interests. Thus when the Khazar state was pummeled in the eighth century by Arab attacks, the trade routes fell into chaos and disruption.

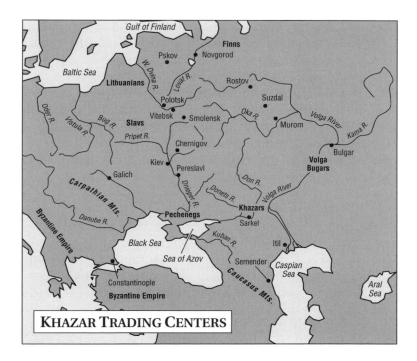

Gulf of Finland

Finns

Pskov • • Novgorod

Baltic Sea

Lithuanians

Rostov

W. Dvina R.

Lovat R.

Polotsk •

Suzdal •

Oder R.

Vistula R.

Bug R.

Slavs

Vitebsk • • Smolensk

Oka R.

Volga River

Kama R.

Pripet R.

Murom •

Chernigov •

Bulgar •

Galich •

Kiev • • Pereslavl

**Volga
Bugars**

Carpathian Mts.

Dnieper R.

Donets R.

Don R.

Volga River

Pecheneҝs

Khazars

Danube R.

Sarkel •

Byzantine Empire

Black Sea

Kuban R.

Itil •

Sea of Azov

Semender •

Caucasus Mts.

Caspian
Sea

Aral
Sea

Constantinople

Byzantine Empire

KHAZAR TRADING CENTERS

THE VARANGIAN PENETRATION

The Scandinavians, who were called Norsemen or Vikings, had begun to raid the southeast coast of the Baltic Sea as early as the sixth century. Their drive for adventure and plunder drew them to explore virtually in all directions, including southeast through the Slavic lands. They were searching for new routes to obtain goods from the Orient, in part because expanding Arab domination of the southern Mediterranean area and Spain in the seventh and eighth centuries had interrupted commercial traffic on those waters.

A vast network of water routes across eastern Europe led to the Black Sea and the Caspian Sea, and to the important market cities on their shores. But each of these routes was from time to time blocked or fiercely guarded by competing tribes, including the Magyars at the mouth of the Dnieper River on the Black Sea, the Pechenegs on the Don River, which empties into the Sea of Azov, and the Bulgars on the Volga River, which connects to the Caspian Sea.

Undeterred, the Varangians, as the Scandinavians were called by the Slavs, persisted in traveling south in their longships (noted for their handling in shallow waters). By 739 they had reached the Black Sea and crossed to the Kuban River valley and the Caucasus Mountains. Varangian traders were to be seen on the streets of Constantinople, the Byzantine capital, and Baghdad, and even in southern and eastern Asia. Hoards of Byzantine coins of the period were brought back to Scandinavia, attesting to the wealth of traders who returned to their homelands. Others settled permanently in Slavic lands and were ultimately assimilated, eventually becoming known by the same name as the Slavic people and the land they occupied, the Rus.

NOVGOROD BELEAGUERED

By the middle of the ninth century, the Khazars were recovering their strength with the help of the Byzantine emperor, who had begun to feel threatened by the Swedish/Slavic state. By 840, the Khazars regained control of the Don and the Donets Rivers, and the entire steppe as far west as the Dnieper River. This loss painfully affected the economic life of the Novgorod area, which, though protected from the Khazars by the thick forests, was dependent on the Oka River region, an area to the south, for grain. Adding to Novgorod's troubles, new bands of Norsemen continued to come ashore in north Russia, only to find the river routes to the south impeded by the Khazars. Frustrated, these warrior seamen began to loot and demand ransoms of the native Slavic population.

Rurik, a Varangian warrior, lands on the Baltic coast. Legend has it that merchants of Novgorod asked Rurik to invade and rule over them.

The pressures of food shortages, loss of trade, and the threat to their security led to civil disorder among the people of Novgorod. According to the *Primary Chronicle,* a twelfth-century document compiled from oral tradition and written fragments: "There was no justice among [the inhabitants of Novgorod], and clan rose against clan; discord thus ensued among them, and they began to make war one against another."[6] No native leader, however, emerged who was strong enough to restore peace.

At least a partial cure for Novgorod's woes arrived in the form of a Dane named Rurik. He had been born in 800 to the clan of Skioldung from Jutland in Denmark. His father had been employed by Charlemagne, the great Frankish king, who had given him estates in Friesland, a northern province of the Netherlands. He established a reputation as an effective warrior from his exploits sailing the Elbe, the Thames, and the Rhine Rivers. According to the *Primary Chronicle,* the merchants of Novgorod singled out Rurik and sent him an invitation: "Our land is great and abundant but there is no order in it; come to rule and reign over us."[7] Although the invitation is probably legendary, Rurik did settle there, and appointed his relatives as barons to reside in nearby towns, subduing independent chieftains in those areas. Other Varangians in Rurik's band seized Kiev from the Khazars in 860, and from there launched an ambitious attack on Constantinople.

OLEG, THE FIRST GRAND PRINCE OF KIEV

Although after a period of years Rurik apparently left Novgorod to reclaim his estates in the Netherlands, his kinsman Oleg reigned in his stead from 882 to 912. Oleg moved the Varangian capital to Kiev, the last fortified point in the forest zone before the Dnieper emerged into the open steppe. Oleg levied tribute on most of the Slav population of the Dnieper area, and he was able to wrest control of the lower Dnieper from the Magyars. The loose federation Oleg established became known as Kievan Rus and extended from the lakes north of Novgorod to south of Kiev.

During the winter, throughout his expanding domain Oleg, now known as the grand prince of Kiev, and his retinue would gather tribute in the form of goods to be sold in Constantinople: mostly furs, beeswax, and honey. In the late spring, as soon as weather permitted, he would lead his troops on the difficult and dangerous journey south to the Black Sea. The precious cargo, accompanied by slaves, merchants, and warriors, was loaded onto large boats, each of which held forty or fifty people. The flotilla sailed down the Dnieper toward the Black Sea and Constantinople. Cargo and barges had to be portaged overland around dangerous rapids, and often into raids and ambushes set by bandits or other tribes, such as the Magyars or the Pechenegs.

Ever desirous of the riches of Constantinople, Oleg tried to conquer that city in 907. Almost fifty years earlier a combined Russian fleet of two hundred boats had been repulsed

Oleg nails his shield to the gate of Constantinople during his attempt to take the city. Although his attack failed, Oleg improved trade relations between Constantinople and Kievan Rus.

before the walls of Constantinople, but not before looting the rich palaces and monasteries outside the city. Oleg's fleet numbered two thousand boats, but was prevented from entering the harbor by an enormous chain. According to the chronicle, Oleg "commanded his warriors to make wheels which they attached to the ships, and when the wind was favorable they spread the sails and bore down on the city from the open country."[8] Although failing to topple Byzantium, Oleg did secure a favorable trade treaty from its emperors, Leo and Alexander. Between the late ninth and mid–eleventh centuries, his successors attacked Byzantium six times; each attack was inconclusive but ended with a trade treaty between Kiev and Byzantium.

SVYATOSLAV'S VICTORIES

Igor, Rurik's son or possibly his grandson, ruled Kiev after Oleg's death, from 913 to 945. He was but one of the Varangian princes in Rus levying tribute on the local population. Though the princes of other towns assembled under Igor's leadership to attack Constantinople, he had no regular authority over them. Two generations after Oleg, the leader of Kiev was named Svyatoslav, a Slavic name, illustrating the assimilation of the Varangians into Slavic culture. Svyatoslav (reigned 962–972) finally broke the power of the Khazars on the steppe, seized the Volga River network from the Bulgars, and penetrated the Balkans, expanding the area paying tribute to him. His gains, however, were temporary, since by weakening the Khazars he lost an important buffer against another, more dangerous enemy, the westward-driving Pechenegs. He met his death at the hands of this warrior band. "The nomads took his head, and made a cup out of his skull, overlaying it with gold, and they drank from it,"[9] according to the *Primary Chronicle*—a fate recalling those who fell to the Scythians so many centuries before.

THE CONVERSION TO THE EASTERN CHURCH

After a relatively brief struggle for power, Vladimir I, a son of Svyatoslav, assumed power over Kievan Rus in 980 and ruled for thirty-five years. Vladimir I had an interest in religion as well as territorial gain. Early in his reign he fostered his ancestors' paganism, based on Perun, the god of thunder; Dashbog, the sun god; and Stribog, the god of winds. But all around him the monotheistic religions had been spreading and paganism was in decline. The Moravians, the Serbs, and the Bulgars converted to the Eastern, or Orthodox, Church; the Poles, the Croats, the Danes, and the Norwegians accepted Roman Catholicism; Islam was spreading in the lands south of the Caspian Sea. Vladimir carefully weighed his options, evidently considering not only the

THE *PRIMARY CHRONICLE*

The *Primary Chronicle,* compiled by Kievan monks beginning in A.D. 1110, is chiefly the story of the first Russian state. It begins like a Russian folktale: "These are the tales of bygone years . . . from whence arose the Russian land." The *Chronicle* includes lives of saints, folk legends, and accounts of battles, as well as the *Instruction of Vladimir Monomakh,* which immortalizes colorful detail from the life of this leader.

The *Primary Chronicle* was imitated all over Russia. Local chronicles from rival towns sometimes provide different views of the same events. The text known as the *Radziwill Chronicle* (because it was once the property of Janusz Radziwill, a Polish prince) was written and beautifully illustrated by fifteenth-century monks, who added to the text of the *Primary Chronicle* a narrative of their own Vladimir-Suzdal region.

characteristics of each religion but also the opportunities for new alliances. Although he had compelling strategic reasons for choosing the Orthodoxy of Constantinople, he was also favorably impressed by the description of Byzantine rituals when his two emissaries returned from a visit to the Church of Hagia Sophia in Constantinople: "We knew not whether we were in heaven or on earth. For on earth there is no such splendor or such beauty, and we are at a loss to describe it." [10]

According to the *Primary Chronicle,* Vladimir's religious conversion prompted him to give up his former life of vice and debauchery and to order the baptism of all his subjects. The first stone cathedral in Russia, the Kievan Church of the Tithe, was completed in 996, and Vladimir supported it with one-tenth of all his revenues. Vladimir's enthusiasm for the new religion met with resistance among his people, however, and as in Europe, pre-Christian beliefs and habits survived for generations, even into the twentieth century. However, Byzantine influence immediately began to shape the development of the visual arts, of architecture, and of social insti-

Vladimir (center) assumed power over Kievan Rus in 980. He is known as St. Vladimir for establishing Christianity in Russia.

THE CYRILLIC ALPHABET

In the ninth century, two Greek brothers, Cyril and Methodius, who were also missionaries, translated parts of the Bible and religious liturgy into a southern Slavic dialect known today as Old Church Slavonic. Since the Slavs had no written language of their own, they invented an alphabet by modifying Greek characters to better represent Slavic articulation.

The establishment of Church Slavonic helped spread literacy in Rus after the conversion to Christianity in 988. However, because the Russian Christians did not have to learn Greek and Latin to read the Bible and liturgy, they were cut off from the classical heritage of the West.

The modern Russian alphabet has thirty-two letters, four fewer than were in use before 1917.

---

tutions such as alms houses, schools, and monasteries. The Cyrillic alphabet, a modified Greek alphabet created by Byzantine missionaries to translate the Scriptures and church liturgy into the Slavic language, gave impetus to the creation of a written history, literature, and law.

KIEV FLOURISHES

Kievan Rus grew into its golden age under Prince Yaroslav, the ruler of the Kievan state from 1036 to 1054. In these important years, Kiev was as large as Paris, with a population of about eighty thousand. Among its artisans were talented mosaists, painters of frescoes and icons, enamelists, jewelers, goldsmiths, wood-carvers, potters, shipwrights, and stonemasons. The structure of society was different from Europe's feudal system, where serfs, or peasant farmers, worked the land as tenants in exchange for services to a noble landowner. In Kievan Rus farmland could be bought, sold, or bequeathed with little restriction, and the serfs, though poor, were free to move around. The prince had his council of advisers, called the duma, who at first were drawn from the military guard but came to include the boyars, the wealthy, landowning aristocrats. All free men could convene the *veche,* or town assembly, by ringing the municipal bell. The decisions of the *veche* had to be unanimous, and violent brawls were typical when an agreement could not be

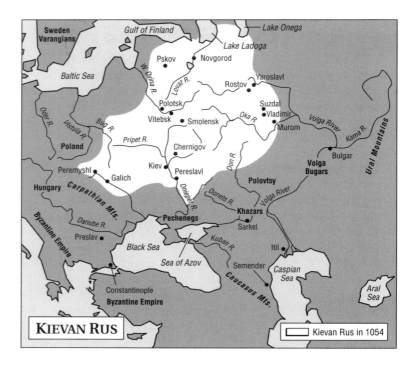

KIEVAN RUS

Kievan Rus in 1054

reached. Power was rooted in the military strength of the prince and his guard, but the *veche* did occasionally rise in revolt against a prince.

Through a series of strategic marriages, Yaroslav was able to bind his family to the royal families of Sweden, Norway, France, Poland, Hungary, and Byzantium, which did much to improve Russia's standing in relation to those nations. At the time of his death, Kievan Rus was a large federation, extending its authority from the Ural Mountains to the shores of the Caspian and Black Seas, to the Gulf of Finland. Despite these achievements, Yaroslav failed to do that which would secure the future for his young state—establish a succession to ensure unity. Instead, he divided his realm among his five sons, sparking intense, destructive feuding for generations.

FEUDS AND FAILURES

Kievan Rus began to falter in the twelfth century, due to several sources of increased instability: raiding nomads of the steppe; a flow of population to the safer, forested northeast region between the Volga and Oka Rivers; internal disputes among the Russian princes; and a decline of trade. A grandson of Yaroslav, Vladimir Monomakh (also known as Vladimir II), was able to hold the bickering principalities in check during his reign, from 1113 to 1125, and is remembered for his personal integrity during these turbulent years. Monomakh left a will including a brief but vivid autobiographical account of his life:

> Among all my campaigns there are 83 long ones, and I do not count the minor adventures. . . . In war and at the hunt, by night and by day, in heat and in cold, I did whatever my servant had to do, and gave myself no rest. . . . I look after things myself and did the same in my own household. . . . I did not allow the mighty to distress the common peasant or the poverty-stricken widow.[11]

A succession of minor princes followed Monomakh; then, in 1169 Kiev was captured not by a foreign invader but by the Russian prince of the northeastern town of Suzdal, Andrei Bogolyubsky, a grandson of Vladimir Monomakh. Bogolyubsky took the title of grand prince and moved his capital to a town called Vladimir, near Suzdal, and also near the newly established town of Moscow. The Novgorod-Kiev trade route had become superfluous to European traders; the successes of the first Crusades and the militant merchants of Venice had diminished Arab domination of the Mediterranean, reestablishing more direct routes between western Europe and the East. As the cities along the middle reaches of the Dnieper lost much of their commercial traffic, the princes turned to the cultivation of land as a more important source of revenue and power.

THE MONGOLS INVADE

Early in the thirteenth century, a new incursion from the steppe brought Russia to its knees. In 1206 a tribal leader named Temuchin, born in northeastern Mongolia, created a confederation of Mongol tribes and took the title of Genghis Khan, meaning "strong ruler," or "prince of all that lies between the oceans." The palace of this ruler was a tent known as a yurt; from this hut of stretched hides, he created a strategy that gained him an enormous empire but wrought a tidal wave of destruction upon China, the Middle East, and Russia. His genius was to fashion an unbeatable military force, composed of divisions of ten thousand brilliantly equipped and trained warriors on horseback. The divisions converged in battles to number one hundred thousand or more. As described by a contemporary in 1243:

> They ride fast bound into their horses, which are not very great in stature, but exceedingly strong, and maintained with little provender [provisions]. They fight constantly and valiantly with javelines, maces, battle-axes and swords. But specially they are excellent archers and cunning warriors with their bows. Their backs are slightly armed, that they may not flee.... Vanquished, they ask no favor, and vanquishing, they show no compassion.... Suddenly diffusing themselves over a whole province, and surprising all the people there unarmed, unprovided, dispersed, they make such horrible slaughters that the king or prince of the land invaded cannot find people sufficient to wage battle against them.[12]

In 1209 Genghis Khan marched south to China, conquering the kingdom of Xi Xia and the empires of the Jin and the

Genghis Khan and his troops show off their superior horsemanship. Khan eventually overran all of central and southern Russia.

Kara Khitai to the west, looting and burning cities, enslaving or slaughtering their inhabitants. Then he sent his armies through central Asia and into Persia, leaving a similar trail of devastation. Several of Genghis Khan's generals and twenty thousand men passed south of the Caspian Sea, crushing two armies in Georgia, and crossed the Caucasus Mountains, defeating a coalition of Turkic tribes on the Russian steppe known as the Polovtsy. In 1223 a combined Russian-Polovetsian force of eighty thousand met the Mongols on the banks of the Kalka River, a tributary of the Don, and fell in confusion and defeat. Several Russian princes were ruthlessly suffocated to death under the table of the Mongols' victory feast.

"REDUCED ALMOST TO NOTHING"

By 1237 the Mongols had ravaged as far west as they ever would, devastating all of central and southern Russia, destroying Kiev, and coming within sixty miles of Novgorod before withdrawing southward. Six years after Kiev's fall to the Mongols, a Franciscan friar described what he saw there:

> When we were journeying through that land we came across countless skulls and bones of dead men lying about on the ground. Kiev had been a very large and thickly populated town, but now it has been reduced almost to nothing, for there are at the present time scarcely two hundred houses there and the inhabitants are kept in complete slavery.[13]

Under the Mongol yoke, as it came to be known, Russia slipped into a pattern of isolation from both western Europe and Byzantium. The incredibly fertile "black earth" steppe had been depopulated by massacre and slavery, and the already weakened former center of Rus, the towns of the river systems, were further undermined. The western border of Rus became more vulnerable to the encroachment of the Hungarians, the Poles, and the Lithuanians. The names of the ancient Slavic tribes disappeared from history.

2

THE SECOND RUSSIA: AN IMPERIAL VISION

After 1240, the whole of Kievan Russia became the western section of the vast Mongol Empire. Only distant Novgorod was spared destruction by the Mongols, who were forced southward before reaching the town because of heavy spring flooding. Nor did the destruction end after the first wave of Mongol invasion. Not only were there numerous uprisings against the Mongols during the era of their rule (1240 to 1480), but the Russians also fought against the Lithuanians, the German crusaders, and the Swedes. The continuous wars, heavy taxation imposed by the Mongols, conscription for life for one out of every ten Russian men into the Mongol military service, outbreaks of plague, and crop failures and resulting famine all contributed to stubborn economic decline. Land and even entire villages were abandoned. Urban handicrafts disappeared. Except in Novgorod and Pskov, the city assembly, the *veche*, also virtually ceased to exist.

The Golden Horde, as the state established by the khan and his entourage became known, settled on the steppe at Sarai (near present-day Volgograd) near the mouth of the Volga River, and from there administered their territories. The Russian princes were required to go to Sarai to make a formal act of obeisance to the khan to receive a *yarlyk*, or edict, authorizing them to collect taxes and rule in their hereditary appanages (districts), in the name of the khan. Uncooperative princes were executed. Practically all contact with western Europe was cut off.

THE RISE OF MOSCOW

At the time of the Mongol invasions, Moscow was a minor city in the principality of Vladimir, so insignificant that Alexander Nevsky, grand prince of Vladimir (1252–1263) assigned it to his youngest son, Daniil. Daniil's son, Ivan I (1325–1340), successfully ingratiated himself with the Mongols and won the *yarlyk* to collect taxes in much of Mongol-dominated Russia. By these riches or by violent acquisition and with the khan's protection, Ivan expanded his appanage fivefold. Moscow's population and prestige also boomed. In 1325 it became the official seat of the Metropolitanate of the Orthodox Church. From this time forward, the interests of Moscow and the Orthodox Church became closely inter-twined, with the church using its moral and economic power and special protected status under the Mongols (church lands and clergy were free of all obligations and tribute) to support the aims of the rulers of Moscow.

Though the personal shrewdness and longevity of Moscow's "bold robbers," [14] as the great Russian historian Kli-uchevsky referred to its early princes, partially explains its swift rise, another prominent factor was Moscow's central lo-cation on river networks. The journey from Moscow to the Baltic, White, Kara, Black, and Caspian Seas could be made entirely by water with a few brief portages, enhancing Moscow's status as a center for communication, whether for trade or war. Surrounded by mostly uninhabited forests, Moscow was also less vulnerable to invasion than were many other urban centers.

MONGOL POWER IN DECLINE

Moscow's expansion in territory and power led to its first challenge to Mongol power in 1378, when Prince Dimitry (1359–1389), a grandson of Ivan I, defeated a small Mongol army and refused to pay the customary tribute. The rulers of the Golden Horde formed an alliance with Moscow's rival Lithuania, to join forces against the Russians. But Dimitry was able to amass an army of 150,000, bolstered by troops of other Russian principalities in a rare instance of mutual co-operation, and engage the Mongols before they reached the Lithuanians. "There was a great slaughter, and a hard battle, and a very great tumult . . . and the blood of both Christians and Tatars [another name for the Mongols] flowed as in a cloudburst, and a great multitude, a countless number, fell dead on both sides," [15] as one chronicle described the Battle of Kulikovo, near the Don River. The cost of the battle was great; Dimitry lost more than 40,000 soldiers and was him-self injured and found half dead on a pile of corpses. The Lithuanians, hearing of the Mongol defeat, chose to retreat to the west. Although two years later the Mongols returned

Dimitry refuses to pay tribute to the Mongols. His action led to the Battle of Kulikovo, a unique event because Dimitry was able to unite several Russian principalities against the Mongols.

to ravage Moscow and central Russia, reimposing the tribute, the Battle of Kulikovo proved to the Russians that the Mongols could be beaten.

Within a generation of Kulikovo, the rule of the Golden Horde was in decline. Vasily I (1389–1425), Dimitry's successor, was able to satisfy the Mongols with gifts in lieu of the full tribute. Further disintegration occurred during the reign of Vasily II (1425–1462), who stopped paying regular tribute in 1452. Eventually, the Golden Horde fragmented into three separate, less formidable units: the Crimean Tatars, the Kazan Khanate, and the Great Horde, the remnants of the Golden Horde. Their despotic system, the subjugation of women, tax collecting, conscription, rule by the knout (a three-branched whip of sharpened rawhide), and the practice of other physical tortures stayed behind in Russia.

When Vasily II died in the old wooden palace of Moscow's Kremlin in 1462, his grand duchy of Moscow [also known as Muscovy] was one of several Russian states and lands. There were two other eastern grand duchies, Tver and Riazan, and a number of small principalities. In the northwest, there were two thriving city-states, Novgorod and Pskov. Novgorod's territories occupied the whole northern part of Russia, from the shores of the Barents Sea, including the northern section of the Ural Mountains, to the lower Ob River in the east. The lands west of Muscovy were under the authority of the Catholic grand dukes of Lithuania and Poland. The middle and lower Volga regions and the southern steppe, still the grazing area of immense herds, were controlled by the hostile Mongol khanates. It fell to Vasily II's son, Ivan III (1462–1505), to accomplish what was benignly referred to in Russia as "the gathering of Russian lands."

THE ERA OF IVAN THE GREAT

Although Ivan III threw off the last vestige of the Mongol yoke in 1480, when the two armies faced off on the Oka River and the Mongols retreated without a battle, it was the remarkable control he gained over his own countrymen that earned him the title "the Great." Through inheritance, confiscation, or forced annexation, most of the remaining independent principalities in eastern Russia accepted Muscovite rule; the few remaining succumbed under his successor, Vasily III (1503–1533).

Ivan III gained the title "the Great" because of his ability to oust the Mongol invaders. He also coined the use of the word "tsar."

In 1472 Ivan III married Sophia Paleologus, a niece of Constantine XI, the last Byzantine emperor (Constantinople fell to the Ottoman Turks in 1453). The marriage brought Byzantine formal customs to the Russian court in Moscow, as well as Byzantine prestige. Ivan added the title of tsar, which was used by the Byzantine rulers to indicate that, like the Roman caesars, they were supreme by divine right.

A new elite social class, the *pomeshchiki,* provided the core of a permanent army and staff for a central administration under Ivan III. By the terms of the *pomeste* system, land was granted to an individual in return for military service; upon his death, the land reverted to the grand prince. Using this system, Ivan intentionally weakened the existing aristocracy, the boyar class, by confiscating their hereditary lands at his whim and giving it to the *pomeshchiks.* Since the *pomeshchiks* did not actually own the land, they could not borrow against it to raise money or make improvements on it to benefit their heirs. The *pomeshchiks* tended to treat the peasants working on the land more harshly. Peasants who found themselves converted into tenants of *pomeshchiks* lost the protection of the communal organizations which had served as buffers between lords and peasants, and they were not likely to obtain assistance from the *pomeshchiks* in hard times.

THE RULE OF IVAN THE TERRIBLE

In 1533 the Muscovite grand princedom passed to three-year-old Ivan IV, with his mother as regent. When she died a few years later (perhaps by poisoning), a vicious struggle for control of the throne by the boyars commenced, which included cruel treatment of the young tsar. "What sufferings did I not endure through lack of clothing and through hunger!" he recalled in a letter composed in adulthood. Vulnerable and unloved in childhood, intent on revenge against the boyars who "with their cunning scheming seized it all,"[16] Ivan IV became known as a perverse sadist who would order savage atrocities, followed by prayers for the salvation of his victims' souls.

At age thirteen, Ivan IV ordered the execution of the leading boyar of the regency. At seventeen he married Anastasia Romanov, the daughter of a boyar, and took the government into his own hands. Ivan IV's reign began with a series of administrative, legal, and military reforms. Some of these changes were aimed at limiting personal freedoms so that people at every level of society would have to serve the tsar unconditionally. With his improved forces, he succeeded in conquering the Tatar khanates of Kazan and Astrakhan, heirs of the Golden Horde, acquiring significant non-Slavic populations and opening the way to Siberia and the east.

After the death of his wife in 1560, Ivan IV apparently suffered a severe emotional collapse. Bloody purges began, directed against the boyars, their servants, and their families. At one point in 1564 he packed up numerous Kremlin treasures and, with a core of retainers, secluded himself in a town sixty miles northeast of Moscow. From there he created an *oprichnina,* effectively a state within a state. He included in the *oprichnina* the territories he considered loyal or vital to him, and also huge boyar domains he intended to confiscate and redistribute, evicting thousands of former tenants. The majority of *oprichniks* were of modest origin or from the *pomeshchiki* class. They became a dreaded secret police, numbering in the thousands. The remainder of the country, the *zemshchina,* was to exist under the status quo. For most of a decade, the *oprichniks* rode through Russia, murdering indiscriminately and dispossessing surviving boyars of their hereditary lands. Not only individuals but entire cities were crushed, including a massacre in Novgorod and another in Moscow.

Ivan IV's *oprichniks* effectively destroyed the political power of the hereditary aristocracy. The most eminent boyars, who before had claimed to share the central authority of the country with the tsar, were gone. But Ivan IV's *oprichniks* left a legacy of immense physical and psychological damage at all levels of society. In the words of Giles Fletcher, an English diplomat in Russia in 1588–1589, "And this wicked policy and tyrannous practice (though now it be ceased) hath so troubled

Ivan the Terrible was a sadist who ordered savage atrocities against his enemies and his "friends" alike. He even murdered his own son.

that country and filled it so full of grudge and mortal hatred ever since, that it will not be quenched (as it seems now) until it burn again in civil flame."[17]

THE TIMES OF TROUBLES

Ivan IV died in 1584, having murdered his only promising son by the same name, leaving behind only a reportedly mentally incompetent son, Fyodor, and Dmitry, an infant by his seventh wife. Boris Godunov, Fyodor's brother-in-law, ruled Russia in the name of Fyodor and tried to stave off a crisis. Upon Fyodor's death, the *zemsky sobor*, the assembly of advisers to the ruler, elected Godunov tsar.

Godunov inherited a shaky state in a period of extreme crisis. Ivan IV's reign of terror had left the country in an economic shambles. The survivors of the old boyar class watched and waited for an opportunity to overthrow Godunov. Widespread crop failures led to famine; there was also an outbreak of plague that wiped out entire villages. As described by a German merchant, Konrad Bussow, who lived in Moscow in these years: "I saw, with my own eyes, people who rolled in the streets and, like animals, ate grass during the summer and hay during the winter. Some of those who died had hay as well as human excrement in their mouths."[18]

Ivan IV's young son Dmitry, who had been living in a small town on the upper Volga, was found dead in 1591, his throat slashed. Several leading boyars accused Godunov of the crime. Decades of rumors, conspiracies, and false pretenders followed. Finally in 1610 Poland and Sweden moved to take advantage of the power vacuum, each advancing their own candidate for Russia's throne. The Poles seized Moscow and Smolensk, and the Swedes occupied Novgorod. Russia was at the point of national disintegration.

The seizure of Moscow and the rallying of the Russian Orthodox Church against the "heretics" of the West provoked a dramatic nationalistic and religious reaction. The people of one small city, Nizhni Novgorod, gave one-third of all their possessions to fund a campaign against the Poles. Other towns and cities followed suit, leading to the formation of a great national army led by Prince Dimitry Pozharsky, which succeeded in wiping out the Polish garrison in Moscow. The army soon convened the *zemsky sobor* for the purpose of

Michael Romanov, first of the Romanov line of tsars, is crowned in 1613. Michael was chosen to be tsar at age sixteen.

electing a tsar. The assembly chose sixteen-year-old Michael Romanov. He was too young to have participated in the years of turmoil, but he was indirectly related to the ancient royal family. His family was held in favor by many factions. Michael Romanov was crowned tsar in 1613. His descendants would rule Russia into the twentieth century.

Michael Romanov (1613–1645) was not an outstanding leader, nor was his son Alexis (1645–1676) or his grandson Fyodor III (1676–1682). However, Russian borders continued to expand, reaching across Siberia all the way to the Pacific by 1689, and the middle and lower Dnieper area of Ukraine, to the west, by 1667. But it was not until 1689, when Peter the Great was old enough to take the throne, that another ruler of vision emerged.

PETER THE GREAT

Peter the Great (1682–1725) is considered by many scholars the most innovative and influential of the tsars. As a boy, during the regency of his elder sister, Sophia, Peter lived in a village outside of Moscow. He became friends with a wide range of people at a time when most Russian royalty led sheltered lives. Contact with tradesmen whetted his appetite for technical competence, which was to become a lifelong passion. Practical, unafraid to shatter traditional institutions, and bent on modernization, his ambition was, in his own words, "to sever the people from their former Asiatic customs and instruct them how all Christian peoples in Europe comport themselves." [19]

Propelled by his desire to learn and with the hope of gaining allies to fight the Turks, in 1697, Peter and 250 companions set out in a "Grand Embassy," to journey through Europe and England. Peter traveled incognito for at least part of the trip (a hard act to pull off, as Peter, at six feet seven inches, towered above most men). He returned to impose new habits and values on his often unreceptive subjects.

RESHAPING THE STATE

Peter the Great's domestic reforms stirred up a lively commotion. Among the profusion of changes by his hand were: developing a new system of central administration; eliminating the office of patriarch of the Orthodox Church and in its stead creating a Holy Synod (essentially a governmental ministry of religion); establishing a learned Academy of Sci-

SIBERIA AND THE EAST

In the sixteenth century, a few wealthy merchant families established prosperous businesses in northern Russia. In time they extended their activities to the Ural area, opening the way to the exploration of Siberia. Motivated by the high prices paid for luxury furs, Russian adventurers traveled farther and farther east into Siberia, searching for new hunting grounds.

By the middle of the seventeenth century, Russians had established their control over all of Siberia except for the Kamchatka Peninsula, which was annexed in 1698. Most of the people living in these regions were members of tribal hunting societies that primarily bred cattle and reindeer, although some practiced agriculture. Though more numerous than the Russian newcomers, the tribes were not united and had no firearms. When they balked against excessive tributes demanded by the Russian Cossacks or other Russian administrative agents, they were crushed.

Gradually over the seventeenth century Russia increased its military presence in Siberia, and also began to develop agriculture and mining. Even so, the sale of furs continued to be the chief source of income from Siberia throughout the seventeenth century.

As early as 1648, criminals were sent to exile in Siberia. From 1729 onward, political prisoners could be banished to this region, known for its harsh climate and sparse development. In the twentieth century, Siberia became synonymous with exile and persecution under the Communist regime. However, after the fall of the Soviet Union, Siberia's reputation has changed, attracting tourists wishing to enjoy the beauty of Siberia's vast sweeps of unspoiled terrain.

ences; reforming the alphabet and the calendar; putting an end to the custom of keeping women in seclusion; founding new schools, libraries, a museum, and a newspaper; and sending hundreds of Russians to study abroad. In an effort to improve communications he built highways and canals. He made diplomatic contact with China, organized the Bering Expedition to discover where or whether America and Asia were joined, and pursued a sea route to India. By the Entailment Law of 1714, Peter changed the class structure of society by creating what historian Fernand Braudel has called a "second aristocracy," giving the *pomeshchiks* and their heirs full possession of the lands they held. And he also ordered the building of a new capital city, St. Petersburg.

MOBILIZED BY WAR

Russia was at war almost continuously during Peter's reign; not surprisingly, many of Peter's efforts were aimed at modernizing the military and forming Russia's first navy. For the first time, promotion within the military depended on merit and not aristocratic privilege; competent commoners could eventually obtain ennoblement via the Table of Ranks established in 1722. Training, drill, and tactics were all updated. Also, modern weaponry was introduced on a wide scale: The pike was abandoned for the bayonet, the flintlock musket replaced the outmoded firelock, and new types of light artillery were brought into service. Peter ordered the construction of factories in the Ural Mountains and near St. Petersburg to keep his troops supplied with munitions.

The enemy was primarily Sweden, which not only controlled the Baltic but also the mouths of most of the great rivers flowing into it, including the Neva, the Duna, the Oder, the Elbe, and the Weser. In 1700, Swedish troops under Charles XII defeated the Russians at Narva, an Estonian city and port. Then in 1707 they left Saxony, where they were camped, to invade Russia. Sweden won an important battle the following year, but instead of marching on Moscow, Charles XII changed his plans and invaded Ukraine. When the Swedes attacked the Russian fortified camp at Poltava, however, the invaders were forced to surrender. Charles XII and a small following escaped over the border into Turkey. Meanwhile, the Russian forces in the Baltic overran the whole Baltic shoreline, from Riga to Vyborg.

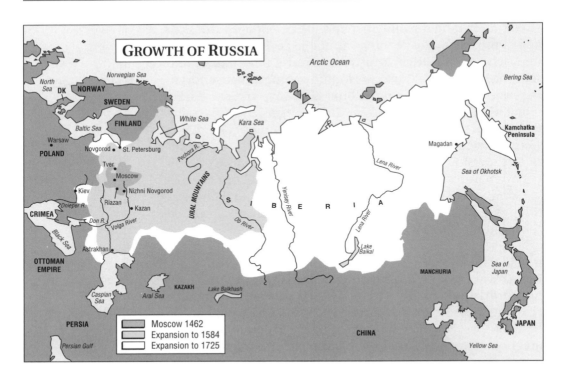

GROWTH OF RUSSIA

Moscow 1462
Expansion to 1584
Expansion to 1725

The defeat of the Swedes at Poltava made a strong impression on Europe: Thereafter, Russia was a power with which Europe had to contend. In 1721, having proved its military strength, Russia annexed parts of Finland, Estonia, and Livonia, assuring its access to the Baltic. From then on, no Russian territory was to be gained by Sweden.

Peter's great energy and vision brought Russia forward, but at a great human cost. The pace of construction in St. Petersburg and the burdens of war were borne most heavily by the people least empowered to resist. "What kind of tsar is he?" asked one villager, as recorded by her interrogators. "He has driven the peasants from their homes and taken our husbands as soldiers. He has made orphans of us and of our children and left us to weep forever."[20] Despite his era of reform, most of Russia still remained a backward, immobilized society. And although an elite group of people supported Peter's innovations, many others resented them and opposed any departure from Muscovite custom. Peter's own son, Alexis, became the hope of conservative elements of society, outraged and alienated by Peter's ways. Alexis became

ST. PETERSBURG

The city of St. Petersburg is perhaps the most visible testimony to Peter the Great's reign. Peter planned his new residence and capital city on this marshy strip of coast on the mouth of the Neva River, seized from Sweden in 1703 during what was called the Great Northern War. The city was oriented to face Europe and the sea, symbolizing Russia's access to the sea and advent as a world power.

Construction began with a fort, and then a shipyard and a network of canals. Government buildings and palaces followed. Unlike Moscow, a walled medieval city, St. Petersburg was carefully designed to include broad plazas and wide streets. Peter commanded the nobility to build handsome mansions according to his architects' plans.

The work was accomplished by tens of thousands of conscripted peasants and convicts. By crude methods they transported the millions of tons of soil required to raise the grade above sea level, clear the forests, level the hills, and dig the canals. The harsh climate and marshy location of the city aggravated the hardships as well as causing the spread of malaria and dysentery. Estimates of deaths of workers vary from thirty thousand to one hundred thousand during the years of the city's construction.

St. Petersburg straddles some 101 islands, and today granite embankments contain the 65 rivers, canals, channels, and streams which separate the islands. From the Admiralty (built in 1705 and replaced between 1806 and 1823 by the present neoclassical structure) on the south embankment, the main streets of the city radiate like spokes of a wheel, crossed by some 365 bridges joining the islands. Some of the great St. Petersburg landmarks include: the Peter and Paul Fortress (construction was begun in 1703 following plans drawn by Peter himself), the Summer Palace, the Winter Palace, the State Hermitage Museum, and the city's most famous statue, the Bronze Horseman (immortalized by Alexander Pushkin's poem of the same name).

Peter the Great founds St. Petersburg. Peter planned the entire city on marshy land and had to transport millions of tons of soil to raise the land above sea level.

embroiled in these disputes and fled abroad. Upon his return to Russia he was arrested and died in prison.

THE EIGHTEENTH CENTURY

Peter the Great failed to name a successor, and his death in 1725 was followed by a series of six rulers in thirty-seven years. The capital rocked with palace revolutions and court intrigues, perpetuating the personal power of the autocrat, or sole source of authority. Yet even with this instability, in war and diplomacy Russia continued to grow stronger. When Catherine II "the Great " (1762–1796) took the throne following the short reign of her unpopular husband, Peter III (1761–1762), Russia reached a pinnacle of international prestige. Russia, Austria, and Prussia presided over the partition of Poland, leading to the return of almost all the Belorussian and Ukrainian lands of the old Kievan state to Russia, and temporarily wiping Poland off the map. Wars with Turkey won Russia control over the northern shores of the Black Sea. Sweden's attack on St. Petersburg was successfully repulsed in 1788–1789.

French became the language of the court and the educated elite, and the aristocracy finally won emancipation from compulsory state service, freeing them to become a more Westernized leisure class. "Nothing can exceed the hospitality of the Russians," exclaimed William Coxe, an English tutor who resided in Russia from 1778 to 1779.

> We could never pay a morning visit to any nobleman without being detained to dinner. . . . The tables were served with great profusion and taste. . . . The plainest as well as the choicest viands were collected from the most distant quarters . . . sterlet from the Volga, veal from Archangel, mutton from Astrakan, beef from the Ukraine, and pheasants from Hungary and Bohemia.[21]

In 1767, following the vigorous suppression of a revolt led by a Cossack leader named Pugachev who promised to liberate the serfs, the oppression of serfdom reached its peak with a decree legalizing punishment by the knout or deportation to Siberia for those who failed to provide "proper submission and absolute obedience in all matters."

Cossacks and peasants were not the only ones to protest serfdom. Widespread fluency in French brought the liberal ideals of the Enlightenment in Europe to the Russian court. Catherine II herself wanted to be known and remembered as an enlightened monarch, and she corresponded with some of the most advanced thinkers of her time, including French writers Voltaire and Diderot. But she was not prepared to make any change in the actual hierarchy of authority advocated by the Russian aristocracy. Appalled by the French Revolution, she broke off diplomatic relations with France, put all French-speaking foreigners under police supervision, and strictly censored the publication of books. In 1790, Aleksandr Radishchev penned the most outspoken criticism of Russian life that had ever appeared in print. His book, *Voyage from St. Petersburg to Moscow,* printed in a limited edition of fifty copies by a small press, described the inhuman practices of marketing serfs, the conditions of forced labor and conscription, the corrupt judges who routinely sold their verdicts, and the equally corrupt merchants. Radishchev was sentenced to death (reduced by Catherine II to ten years' exile in Siberia). His legacy was a new political and intellectual elite: the disaffected intelligentsia.

By presiding over the partition of Poland, Catherine II was able to negotiate the return of nearly all the Belorussian and Ukrainian lands of Old Kiev to Russia.

THE NINETEENTH CENTURY

Already a multinational and multireligious state by 1800, Russia became larger and even more diverse in the nineteenth century. Finland was annexed from Sweden in 1809, Bessarabia from Turkey in 1812, and central Poland, including Warsaw, in 1815. The lands of the Caucasus Mountains, including Georgia, Armenia, and Azerbaijan, were incorporated by 1859.

Russian patriotism had been boosted by the experience of French emperor Napoléon I's ruinous march to Moscow and his army's famous retreat, depicted by Leo Tolstoy in his epic novel *War and Peace.* But officers and conscripted commoners alike were disappointed to return from their eye-opening experiences in the Napoleanic Wars in western Europe to conditions of repression at home. After the death of Alexander I (1801–1825), his brother, Nicholas I (1825–1855), was immediately faced with the first conspiracy in Russia to overthrow the tsar. The revolutionaries, who became known

SERFDOM FOR MOST RUSSIANS

The power and wealth of the landholding aristocracy depended upon the labor of the farmers living on the estates. During the centuries following the Mongol period the peasants, who were known as serfs, became legally bound to the land they were living on. They were bought, sold, and generally treated as property by their owners. The serfs' obligations to their landlords included not only their labor but also cash payments and produce from the land. These obligations were often paid collectively by the peasant *mir,* or commune, so that if any individual peasant or peasant family fell short, the entire group had to share the loss.

Since there were no laws limiting the demands on serfs, the conditions of their daily lives varied widely from a state of destitution to a minimum level of comfort. New owners of land had no legal obligation to keep serf families intact.

It was difficult and expensive but still legally possible for serfs to move from one estate to another during the three-week period around St. George's Day (November 25) until 1649. At that time, this last vestige of freedom left over from Kievan times was lost with the passage of a new set of laws. Peasants could no longer move by their own volition. The Code of 1649 affected some 12 million people, over 90 percent of the population. Many townspeople also became similarly bound, under threat of torture, exile, or death. Hundreds of peasants, sometimes whole villages, fled to the frontiers of Siberia or to the great rivers of the south to join the Cossack groups, producing labor shortages and a tightening of efforts to recover them.

An artist's rendition of a typical living room of a Russian peasant's house on the Kara Sea coast.

as the Decembrists (after the month their plot was launched), were a mixed group of intellectuals, idealistic military officers, and aristocrats. Though essentially disorganized and lacking public support, they incited the soldiers of some imperial guards to revolt. The movement, however, was summarily crushed, its leaders either hanged or exiled.

But change was coming, just the same. As Aleksandr Herzen, a radical journalist and essayist, wrote in the 1830s: "A new world was pushing at the door, and our hearts and souls opened wide to meet it." [22] The economic base was gradually shifting to urban centers. In 1864 there were three times as many towns with a population of over fifty thousand as in 1830. In general, the population doubled between 1800 and 1860, when it reached 76 million. But still, about four-fifths of the population were serfs, whether in servitude to nobles or the state. Revolts in agricultural districts increased, numbering as many as 556 during Nicholas I's reign. To deal with the unrest, a department known as the Third Section was created, which functioned as a repressive police force to persecute troublemakers.

Although Russia was developing industrially, it was falling behind other powers at an alarming rate. For instance, in 1850 Russia had only five hundred miles of railroad compared to eighty-five hundred miles in the United States. Lack of technological prowess inhibited the Russian military in the Crimean War (1853–1856). Russian soldiers lost battles in which they far outnumbered the enemy because of inefficiency, corruption, and a critical lack of adequate transportation, communications, and supplies. At the conclusion of the war, having suffered great loss of life, Russia forfeited the mouth of the Danube, parts of Bessarabia, and earlier conquests in the Caucasus to Turkey. In addition, Russia had to renounce future ambitions against Turkey and remove warships and fortifications from the Black Sea, a severe blow to a country in critical need of ice-free ports. These disappointments, a soaring state deficit, and a new wave of peasant unrest forced Alexander II (1855–1881) to come up with a policy of reform.

ALEXANDER II'S LIBERAL PROGRAM

At the conclusion of the Crimean War, Tsar Alexander II announced to representatives of the nobility, "It is better to begin to destroy serfdom from above, than to wait until that

Alexander II wanted to reform the institution of serfdom; however, his Emancipation Manifesto did little to improve the lives of most serfs.

time when it begins to destroy itself from below."[23] Still, it took years of discussion to finish the Emancipation Manifesto, which was read from the pulpits of Russia's churches in 1861. The law itself comprised nearly four hundred pages of complex and sometimes contradictory provisions. Finally, peasants were freed from servitude. But to many, the terms of this freedom were onerous: Land was allotted to village communes, or *mir*, not individuals, to be redistributed every ten years. And a peasant could buy only half the land he had previously cultivated, for annual "redemption" payments over forty-nine years which most could not hope to afford. The tsar's regime was ready for their protests: Peasants who rioted were shot down on village streets, flogged, or sent into exile to Siberia.

Other reforms had far-reaching implications. The judicial system became a separate branch of government. In 1874 military service was reorganized and the length of service reduced from twenty-five to six years, compulsory for all males at the age of twenty, with exceptions. On the local level, elected rural councils, *zemstva*, were made responsible for local education, medical care, and road building, and were empowered to levy local taxes. Similar provisions created elective town councils.

The reforms stopped short of granting a constitution, which frustrated the aims of young, educated radical groups. One such group, called the *Narodnaya Volya*, the People's Will, led by Alexander Ulyanov (the older brother of Lenin, who would figure so prominently in the next generation of revolutionaries), succeeded in assassinating Alexander II as he rode through St. Petersburg in an open carriage in 1881.

THE EMPIRE APPROACHES 1900

As the century closed, Russia achieved some milestones in development, including the construction of the Trans-Siberian railroad, providing a military link to Asiatic Russia and facilitating overall economic development. There was also remarkable growth in mining, metallurgical, textile, and chemical industries, and the Baku oil fields were second in production only to those in Texas. Much of this was masterminded by Sergei Witte, a minister in Alexander III's government (1881–1894) who oversaw the planning and financing of what was called "state capitalism," large-scale business development initiated by the state rather than private individuals or corporations. Despite these rapid changes, Russia still lagged behind the United States, Great Britain, Germany, and France in industrial and manufacturing power. Some 80 percent of the population derived its livelihood from agriculture, and although agricultural output was increasing, it was outstripped by the pace of population growth. In the cities, many workers had to contend with poor housing, unsanitary living conditions, and deadly outbreaks of disease. The majority of industrial workers were also seasonal farm laborers, and moved between town and country.

Both Alexander III and Nicholas II (1894–1917) believed devoutly in the virtues of autocracy, and both looked to scapegoats, such as the Jewish population, to explain Russia's difficulties. From 1881 onward, as a deliberate tool of state policy, there was a series of ruthless pogroms against the Jews within the Pale, the restricted area of Jewish settlement in modern Belarus and Ukraine. As a result of this activity, and the medieval-style expulsions of Jews from Moscow and Kiev, over a million of the 6 million Jews in Russia emigrated, largely to North America.

Other groups suffered as well, under the policy of "Russification," which vigorously suppressed all languages and traditions other than Russian. What remained of local autonomy in Russian-occupied Finland, Poland, Baltic states, Ukraine, and Armenia was destroyed. Religious nonconformists risked deportation and imprisonment. Repressive internal security measures included a ban on trade unions and political parties, and military control of the judiciary. The government also tightened control over the spread of ideas at every level of society, from village schools to universities to newspapers.

TURMOIL GROWS

In 1904 war broke out against Japan over the conflict of Russian and Japanese aspirations in Asia. The war turned out disastrously for the Russians. In 1905 the Russians were overcome by the Japanese at Mukden, in Manchuria, after a long battle that claimed some two hundred thousand lives. After

Cossack raiders are driven out of Manchuria by the Japanese during the Russo-Japanese War, a devastating failure for Russia.

a long cruise around Africa, the Russian Baltic fleet was destroyed in the great naval battle of Tsushima. Hostile public opinion generated by this war contributed to the growing turmoil of revolutionary activity in Russia.

On Sunday, January 22, 1905, a great procession of workers under the leadership of Father George Gapon marched to the tsar's palace in St. Petersburg. They intended to present a petition asking for political freedom, equality before the law, lower taxes, and better working conditions. In the absence of Nicholas II, the marchers met with gunfire. "Bloody Sunday" ended with the murder of two hundred and the wounding of eight hundred more defenseless, singing petitioners, many of them carrying icons and portraits of the tsar. A wave of strikes and mutinies in the army and navy followed. From this fateful day, the autocracy was doomed: The spark of revolutionary fervor had been lit and would soon flame across Russia.

THE THIRD RUSSIA: THE COMMUNIST VISION

The spontaneous, widespread rebellion that began with Bloody Sunday became known as the 1905 Revolution. The generation of trained, radical revolutionaries who were to augment and steer these forces by 1917 were by no means in charge of the events of 1905.

The revolutionaries needed the 1905 "dress rehearsal," as the pivotal revolutionary leader Leon Trotsky was to call it, to further their development, both philosophically and pragmatically. Since the 1860s, clandestine organizations had focused on overturning the absolute monarchy. But whereas the first wave of revolutionaries strove to politicize the peasantry and tended to idealize rural life and the spirit of equality of the peasant *mir*, the second wave, informed by the writings of German political philosopher Karl Marx, found the old, rural ways distasteful. Instead, they looked to the revolutionary potential of urban workers and were advocates of modernization, which they saw as part of a historical cycle. According to Marxist prediction, the first revolution would be propelled by the bourgeoisie (property-owning middle class) overthrowing the aristocracy. The proletariat (the class, according to Marx, that lives by selling its labor and is exploited by capitalist society) revolution could occur only after capitalism had run its course.

REVOLUTIONARY POLITICS TAKE SHAPE

The Social Democratic Labor Party, formed in 1898, split into two factions in 1903. The group known as the Mensheviks (meaning minority) supported a broadly based open party and sought to replace the autocracy with a democratic constitution. The Bolsheviks (meaning majority), led by the revolutionary Vladimir Ilyich Ulyanov, who had changed his name to Lenin, believed that the workers

Vladimir Ilyich Ulyanov (Lenin) led the Bolsheviks to victory during the Russian Revolution.

required professional revolutionaries to promote their interests and speed the coming revolution. Fearing that the lack of democratic process in Bolshevik philosophy would lead to a one-man dictatorship, Leon Trotsky, who had risen to lead the St. Petersburg Soviet (the Russian word for council, but essentially, the strike committees that sprang up to coordinate revolutionary activity), sided with the Mensheviks.

The first Duma, authorized by Tsar Nicholas II in 1905, convened in April 1906, but the assembly was dismissed after 73 days, its demands for reform unacceptable to the tsar's government. In January 1906 the tsar had issued the new Fundamental Law of the Empire, which confirmed the supreme autocratic power of the tsar and reversed concessions made in 1905. The second Duma met in 1907 and disbanded after 102 days. A third Duma managed to serve out its full five-year term from 1907 to 1912 . But a separate Imperial State Council, established in 1906 and drawn from the privileged classes, regularly upset initiatives for change emanating from the Duma and its supporters.

WAR IN EUROPE

In Europe, a rapid shift in the balance of power between nations had serious repercussions. Under the guidance of Prime Minister Otto von Bismarck, Germany had united and rapidly grown in industrialization, military power, and population, surpassing both Britain and France. New alliances began to form. The ties between France, Britain, and Russia were strengthened by the signing of the so-called triple entente in 1907 to assure their mutual defense in the case of German aggression. Germany grew closer to Austria, with which it had established secret and public alliances since the 1870s. In 1908 Austria-Hungary (the two states were ruled together by the Hapsburg monarchy from 1867 to 1918) annexed the Turkish provinces of Bosnia and Herzegovina. Serbia, a Slavic nation, also broke away from Turkey, declaring independence on the presumption Russia would step in to protect it. The chief threat to Serbia was Austria-Hungary, which wanted to discourage Slavic nationalism because of Slavic populations within its own borders. Thus when a

Serbian revolutionary assassinated the heir to the Austrio-Hungarian throne in Sarajevo in 1914, Austria-Hungary declared war on Serbia. Germany declared war on Russia, and Britain and France responded likewise against Germany. World War I had begun.

Tsar Nicholas II sent millions of men to the German border and installed himself in army headquarters near the fighting. As the opposing armies engaged in intense and inconclusive fighting with enormous casualties on both sides, the tsarina, Alexandra, Nicholas's beloved wife and daughter of a German duke, was in de facto control of the government back in St. Petersburg, now called Petrograd. Alexandra's chief adviser was a mystic known as Rasputin, who had gained influence with the royal family on the basis of his controlling their son's hemophilia with hypnosis. Rasputin exploited the situation to satisfy his own desire for power. Under his sway, the tsarina nominated and fired ministers and governors in such quick succession that instability became the norm.

As the war dragged on, economic conditions worsened. In the winter of 1914–1915, the Russian army went without essential military supplies; half of the reinforcements sent to the front had no rifles. Inflation and food shortages began to affect urban populations.

THE FINAL DAYS OF TSARISM

Meanwhile, speeches in the Duma in 1916 became more impassioned. The pressure intensified when a breakdown in the

Russian soldiers march against the Germans in World War I. Although often ill equipped and poorly trained, the Russian army had the advantage of sheer numbers.

After refusing to fire on protesting civilians, soldiers march to the Duma with a banner inscribed with the words "Down with Monarchy! Long Live the Democratic Republic!"

After refusing to fire on protesting civilians, soldiers march to the Duma with a banner inscribed with the words "Down with Monarchy! Long Live the Democratic Republic!"

chaotic food supply system caused massive bread shortages in early March 1917. People filled the streets of Petrograd, sacking food stores and shouting "Down with the autocracy!" and "Down with the war!" The turning point came when orders to use force against the demonstrators were disobeyed and a mutiny took place in a regiment of the imperial guard. The Duma refused Nicholas's order to dissolve, and it instead formed an executive committee to serve as a "provisional" government until a truly representative national assembly could meet. The provisional government, a group of liberal aristocrats and middle-class leaders, included only one socialist.

When Nicholas II tried to return to the capital from the front, he could find no loyal troops; all his ministers had been arrested by the "Provisional Committee of the Duma." The end had come. On March 15, 1917, Nicholas abdicated, concluding three centuries of rule by the Romanov dynasty.

THE BIRTH OF THE SOVIET SYSTEM

Another development with enormous repercussions began to take shape. The decision-making authority of the rapidly expanding Petrograd Soviet quickly became concentrated in the Executive Committee, the Ispolkon, which made its headquarters in the same building as the Duma, the Taurida Palace. The fledgling provisional government turned to the Ispolkon for support. Almost at once, the Ispolkon grasped legislative powers for itself, defying the provisional government. Hardly more than a week after the provisional government had come into being, the minister of war wrote in a letter, "The Provisional government has no real power of any kind and its orders are carried out only to the extent permitted by the Soviet of Workers' and Soldiers' Deputies, which controls the most essential strands of actual power, inasmuch as the troops, railroads, and postal services are in its hands."[24]

The February Revolution, as it is called (because by the Julian calendar, which was in place in Russia until 1918, Nicholas had abdicated in February, not March), was a genuine revolution in that public disorder brought down the tsarist regime and replaced it with a provisional government. The October Revolution of 1917, however, was actually a coup d'etat, carefully staged by Lenin and his Bolshevik followers.

Lenin, who had been in exile in Switzerland during the war, reentered Russia with the aid of the German government (Russia's enemy in the war) in April 1917. Lenin advocated withdrawing from the war so that the next phase of the revolution as he saw it—civil war—could transpire. In a shocking speech at the All Russian Bolshevik Conference in Petrograd, Lenin opposed any support to the provisional government. The bourgeois phase of the revolution had to transform into a socialist revolution in a matter of weeks, not years. A Menshevik in the audience later wrote:

> I cannot forget that speech, like a flash of lightning, which shook and astonished not only me, a heretic accidentally thrown into delirium, but also the true believers. . . . The spirit of universal destruction, which knew no obstacles, no doubts, neither human difficulties nor human calculations, circled in Kshesinskaia's hall above the heads of the exchanged disciples.[25]

Lenin's program included the transfer of all power to the Soviets, confiscation of all private land, integration of all financial resources into a national bank under Soviet supervision, and Soviet control of all production and distribution. The Germans, seeing how destabilizing Lenin's goals were, were delighted. Their agent in Stockholm cabled Berlin, "Lenin's entry into Russia successful. He is working exactly as we desire."[26]

THE FAILURE OF THE PROVISIONAL GOVERNMENT

Aleksandr Kerensky, a leading member of the Petrograd Soviet as well as the provisional government, became prime minister in July 1917. Kerensky's hope was that victory over the Germans could be achieved, and he ordered a last great offensive to achieve this aim. Anarchy and civil war descended upon Russia as German troops threatened Petrograd. The Russian troops were divided among those loyal to the provisional government and those who thought the provisional government incapable of restoring order. Meanwhile, the provisional government could neither pursue the war nor withdraw from it. Finally, by September 1917, empowered by large funds channeled to him by the Germans, Lenin's virulent campaign against the government and the war began to pay off. Lenin formed a private army, called the Red Guard, and bombarded its ranks with propaganda.

Kerensky now made a fateful mistake. Suspicions of General Lavr Kornilov's personal ambitions provoked Kerensky to dismiss Kornilov as commander in chief of the Russian forces. Kornilov was a popular commander, and Kerensky's confused actions estranged the provisional government from the military, liberals, and conservatives. The Bolsheviks gathered more momentum, and in municipal elections held in August they made dramatic gains, winning majorities in both the Petrograd and Moscow Soviets.

THE BOLSHEVIK COUP

Leon Trotsky, who joined the Bolshevik Party following the February Revolution, and who was also head of the Petrograd Soviet, planned and executed the final coup. The first

Aleksandr Kerensky (center) became prime minister of Russia in July 1917, but he lost power to the Bolsheviks a few months later.

The Red Guards, composed of civilians who seized all available guns, take control of the Winter Palace in Petrograd in support of the Bolsheviks.

step was to gain control of the 240,000 soldiers in the capital and its environs. This was accomplished on November 5 by convincing the military units to support the Milrevkom (Military-Revolutionary Committee) created by the Petrograd Soviet to defend Petrograd from an expected German invasion. Unbeknownst to many, the Milrevkom's program had significantly extended to defense against "counterrevolution," or opposition within Russia. Over the next few days, the Bolsheviks methodically took control of all key government buildings. Little blood was shed; the provisional government could summon no military support. The Red Guards seized the Winter Palace and arrested the members of the provisional government, although Kerensky escaped in a car lent by the U.S. embassy.

In other cities, the Bolsheviks gained control under a variety of scenarios. By late November, the new government controlled the heartland of the Russian empire. Most ordinary people had no idea that power had passed to an armed committee determined to exercise it without limit.

Although the Bolsheviks had demanded a constituent assembly when the provisional government was in power, when elections were actually held in late November 1917, it became clear that their rivals, members of the Socialist Revolutionary Party, were in the legitimate position of assuming power. The Constituent Assembly opened in January 1918. After one day, Lenin posted his private guards around the Taurida Palace, preventing entry. He had no intention of ruling by coalition, and he instead opened a counterassembly, the Third Congress of Soviets, where Bolshevik power was absolute. In Lenin's own words, "The dispersal of the Constituent Assembly by Soviet authority was the complete and candid liquidation of formal democracy in the name of revolutionary dictatorship."[27] Lenin's new government dropped "provisional" from its name and established itself as the permanent government of Russia and its possessions.

THE END OF THE WAR

In 1918, Lenin negotiated the end of the war between Russia and Germany. Under the Brest-Litovsk Treaty, named for the Polish town where the peace conference was held, Russia gave up all claim to Poland, Finland, Ukraine, Lithuania, Latvia, Estonia, and Transcaucasia. The reduced Soviet state had given up nearly a third of the empire's agricultural land, half its industry, four-fifths of its mines, and a third of its population. Lenin was willing to accept such losses because of his fervent belief that the territory would be recouped once workers throughout the rest of Europe joined Russia in a communist revolution.

Lenin still had to face anticommunist (or White) forces who opposed the Bolsheviks. But the White armies, supplied by the Allies (mainly France, Great Britain, and the United

Lenin speaks before troops in Red Square in 1919. Lenin led his troops to victory over the White, or anticommunist, forces who opposed him.

States), were scattered geographically and lacked a unified command and program. The Bolsheviks never lost Moscow, Petrograd, or the railroad system, which gave them a logistical superiority.

In the course of the civil war, the governments of Ukraine, Belorussia, and Transcaucasia (including Georgia, Armenia, and Azerbaijan) were persuaded to join Lenin's union. Together with the Soviet Federated Socialist Republic (Russia) they formed the Union of Soviet Socialist Republics (USSR) in 1922.

THE DICTATORSHIP TAKES ROOT

Finally, Lenin and the Bolsheviks had Russia as their giant laboratory to practice what they called "genuine communism." In an effort to liquidate the market, the heart of a capitalist system, they abolished private property and purposefully fostered inflation to make money worthless (a Marxist utopian goal was a moneyless economy). Industrial and agricultural production fell dramatically, and a devastating famine in 1921–1922 caused starvation and ruin. Meanwhile the bureaucracy in charge of industry grew by leaps and bounds. Lenin was forced to step back from "war communism," as these economic policies were dubbed in 1921 to excuse their failure, and to replace it with the "new economic policy," which allowed for a less-restricted economy.

Another assault on the population took place at the hands of a secret police, the Cheka, which had been formed in 1918 to arrest political opponents. The Cheka was modeled after the tsar's Department of Police and staffed with hardened outcasts who had no qualms about the use of terror. After an attempt on Lenin's life in 1918, the Cheka was freed to pursue a policy of merciless and indiscriminate destruction known as the Red Terror. Estimates of the number of victims range from 50,000 to 140,000.

Law as such had ceased to exist on November 22, 1917, when Lenin dissolved nearly all the courts and abolished the legal professions. They were replaced by "people's courts" and "revolutionary tribunals," in which justice was subservient to the government's will. Among the victims of this lawless society were the deposed tsar, his wife, children, and domestic staff, who in 1918 were shot dead in the middle of the night by the local Cheka near their place of incarceration in Siberia.

THE KGB

The first institution founded under Lenin's regime after the October Revolution was the political police, commonly known by its abbreviated Russian name, the Cheka. Its purpose was to fight "counterrevolution" and sabotage of Bolshevik goals. An agency of political repression, it used terror as a means of eliminating opposition. It also established concentration camps, internal security camps, and censorship of the press.

In later years, its purpose unchanged, the Cheka became known successively as the GPU, the OGPU, the NKVD, the MVD, and finally, the KGB (the Committee for State Security). The KGB was also responsible for foreign espionage. Loss of employment, eviction from housing, threats to family members, and blackmail were typical techniques employed against Soviet citizens in the KGB's surveillance mission to protect the USSR from real or imagined enemies.

In 1921, at the Communist Party Congress (as the Bolshevik Party had been renamed in 1918), Lenin made it clear that the Party would not put up with internal dissension, and the Central Committee could expel anyone from the Party. Concentration camps that appeared towards the end of 1918 contained more than seventy thousand prisoners by 1923.

FROM LENIN TO STALIN

Lenin died in 1924 at the age of fifty-four after a series of debilitating strokes. The Bolshevik state he designed in many ways resembled Russia under tsarist rule. By the "universal labor obligation" of 1918, every citizen had to work for the state, under threat of execution. For peasants, that included forced labor with no compensation. No inhabitant was allowed to leave the country without permission. The Communist bureaucracy, like the tsar's regime, stood above the law.

Joseph Stalin, the son of a Georgian shoemaker, had risen in the Bolshevik Party under Lenin. By 1922 Stalin was the only official who belonged to all three of the ruling organs of the Central Committee of the Communist Party: the Politburo (the chief policy-making committee), the Orgburo (the agency in charge of Party personnel and organization), and the Secretariat (which oversaw the work of the departments of the Central Committee). Thus he supervised the staffing of virtually all branches of the Party and government. After Lenin's death, Stalin used gangster tactics to gain an iron grip on the Central Committee of the Communist Party. Although he held no state office until 1940, he quickly consolidated power in political, military, and economic affairs, accompanied by the murder, execution, or exile of all his opponents.

RUTHLESS COLLECTIVIZATION

Stalin's plan for rapid social and economic transformation of the country hinged on forced collectivization of all farmland, beginning in 1929. Between 1929 and 1931, as part of the First Five-Year Plan instituted in 1928, 20 million individual farms were reorganized into 250,000 collectives. The effect on agricultural production was disastrous. The heaviest losses occurred in Ukraine, where collectivization was used to crush vestiges of Ukrainian nationalism. The new laws required that no grain from a collective farm could be given to members of the farm until the government's quota was met. This policy and its implementation under Stalin condemned millions of peasants to death by starvation. Even seed grain was forcibly confiscated. Any man, woman, or child caught taking even a handful of grain from a collective farm could be executed or deported. Peasants were also forcibly prevented from leaving their villages. Collectivization was "probably the most massive warlike operation ever conducted by a state against its own citizens,"[28] according to one historian. The death toll from the 1932–1933 famine in the Ukraine has been estimated at 6 to 10 million.

Joseph Stalin believed that his Five-Year Plans, which were implemented using communist collectivist principles, would bring rapid industrialization to Russia.

The First Five-Year Plan also launched a program of unprecedented industrial investment. Coal production more than tripled between 1928 and 1938, and the production of iron and steel expanded fourfold. Projects included the Dnieper Dam of 1932, the Stalingrad tractor factory, a steel plant in the Urals, and new mines and machine industry in Siberia. The railroads in 1938 were carrying five times as much freight as in 1913. But frequently, the price of these gains was human suffering on a mass scale, since they were built wholly or in part by slave labor.

As one witness described, "Men froze, hungered and suffered, but the construction work went on." [29]

RULE BY EXILE AND PURGE

Beginning in 1936, Stalin instigated a series of show trials, executions, and political purges. Millions of Soviet citizens were sent to a network of prison camps, known as the Gulag Archipelago, which extended across northern Russia into Siberia. There inmates labored under appalling living conditions. Those unable to work were executed en masse. It is estimated that 10 million people were arrested and 3 million executed before 1941.

Outside of Russia, the extent of Stalin's system of tyranny remained scarcely known. Even the famine of 1932–1933, the worst in Russian history, was unreported at the time. Those who traveled to Russia were either duped by Soviet propaganda or bribed by the Soviet regime.

Despite his paranoid distrust of everyone around him, including his closest associates and family, the one person Stalin apparently trusted was Adolf Hitler, the leader of Nazi Germany, who had risen to power in 1933 by proclaiming the German people a "master race" destined to rule all of Europe. In 1939, Stalin signed a secret nonaggression pact with Germany whose provisions divided Poland between the two countries and promised Estonia, Latvia, and Finland to Russia. When Germany invaded Poland a week later, France

Joseph Stalin (second from right) and other officials watch as Soviet foreign minister Molotov signs a non-aggression treaty between the Soviet Union and Germany.

and Great Britain declared war. Though Russia remained neutral, Stalin's armies moved into eastern Poland, destroying towns and villages and brutally murdering fifteen thousand Polish officers. Stalin also secured Latvia, Estonia, and Lithuania, where resistance was ineffective. In November 1939 the Soviets invaded Finland. Despite warnings about Hitler's intentions, Stalin refused to build up Russia's forces against Germany, even insisting that artillery fire was not to be returned. He wanted to give Germany no pretext to attack. At the same time, Russia sold resource-starved Germany valuable grain, oil, aircraft fuel, iron ore, manganese, and cotton in exchange for weapons and naval blueprints. All over the world, Communist Party branches reversed their anti-Nazi stance.

THE USSR ENTERS WORLD WAR II

However, in 1941 Hitler evidently surprised Stalin by ordering the invasion of Russia in a three-pronged offensive directed towards Leningrad (the former Petrograd) in the north, Moscow in the center, and Ukraine in the south. What Stalin did not realize was that the attack was part of Hitler's program all along: He wanted to destroy the Soviet Union to get rid of "Jewish" Bolshevism, as he called it, despite the fact that Stalin's Russia was as anti-Semitic as Russia under tsarism. Also, given Germany's dependence on imported raw materials for industrial production and modern weaponry, the conquest and plunder of Russian lands and control of Russia's Ukrainian breadbasket had great appeal for Hitler's Reich. Fierce battles in the heart of Russia followed. Leningrad was under siege for two and a half years, during which it is estimated that a million and a half of its inhabitants either were killed in the fighting or died of starvation. Moscow, the second-prong target, was not taken, and the Soviet regime succeeded in evacuating industrial facilities to the Ural Mountains, out of reach of the enemy. The output from these transplanted factories, together with material aid supplied by the Allies (mainly the United States and Great Britain), helped ensure that the Soviet forces were better armed and equipped than the Germans.

The Battle of Stalingrad (Volgograd) was a turning point in the war. After this German defeat, the Russians swept westward and southward into Romania, Bulgaria, the Baltic

Soviet troops, dressed in winter gear, fight German invaders during World War II.

states, Poland, Hungary, Austria, and Czechoslovakia. On April 22, 1945, Soviet forces surrounded Berlin and linked up with American troops on the Elbe River in Germany. Hitler committed suicide, and the German government surrendered on May 8, 1945.

Although the Soviet Union was fully involved in fighting the Germans and suffered high casualties (an estimated 20 million Soviet citizens lost their lives), it had not joined the Allies in the war against Japan. Stalin finally declared war on Japan two days after an atomic bomb was dropped on Hiroshima, on August 6, 1945. He then sent troops across the Soviet border into Manchuria. Only minor skirmishes took place, and on August 14 Japan quit the war.

THE COLD WAR

The world community was greatly shaken by World War II. First, the war and the newly unleashed destructive power of the atomic bomb had caused immense loss of life. Second, the Holocaust, humanity's first "industrial" genocide, in which an estimated two-thirds of Europe's Jewry were destroyed (including a million Ukrainian Jews), loomed as an immense human tragedy. And finally, the two opposite poles of social organization—the free market and private capital system versus the controlled economy and state-owned capital system—quickly aligned world politics into an emerging competition. In this atmosphere, the postwar world began to take shape. The Soviet Union took control of the governments of Lithuania, Estonia, Moldavia, Poland, Czechoslovakia, Hungary, Romania, and Bulgaria, sweeping an additional 100 million people under Soviet domination.

Stalinist repression began anew. Critics were banished to the Gulag, including young Aleksandr Solzhenitsyn, who survived to describe the Gulag system in great detail, eventually winning the Nobel Prize for literature. Stalin isolated the "Eastern bloc" nations from the rest of the world behind what British statesman Winston Churchill called the "iron curtain."

In 1949, nine nations of Western Europe plus the United States, Britain, and Canada formed the North Atlantic Treaty

Organization (NATO) to insure a united response to communist Russia, which had by that year developed its own atomic bomb. In 1955 the Soviet Union consolidated its existing network of military alliances into the Warsaw Mutual Defense Pact, formalizing the cold war. Around the world the Soviet Union supported communist revolutionaries, while the United States backed anticommunist forces—the nuclear arsenals of both powers hovering over each unfolding drama.

Stalin died on March 5, 1953. It took years before his crimes would be fully examined in Russia and exposed to the outside world. The next generation of leaders would all be tainted by their association with Stalin, though they tried to distance themselves from his policies.

THE KHRUSHCHEV ERA

Nikita Khrushchev emerged from the struggle for power following Stalin's death to become first secretary of the Central Committee of the Communist Party in 1953. Although he had participated in the purges under Stalin, in 1956 he denounced Stalin's "cult of personality" (the term used for the deluge of propaganda idolizing Stalin). Khrushchev also criticized the execution and imprisonment of Party members, although he did not denounce crimes against non–Party members. Nonetheless, his speech was a breakthrough and contributed immediately to a freer intellectual atmosphere in the Soviet Union and Eastern Europe. From that moment, a shift began to take place with regard to Stalin's place in Soviet history. In 1961 Stalin's body was removed from the mausoleum he shared with Lenin in Moscow's Red Square, places named after Stalin were renamed, and eventually thousands of political prisoners were released.

For ordinary Russian citizens, the 1950s and 1960s were a time of relative peace and rising living standards. Khrushchev gave special attention to agriculture, saying, "You cannot put theory into your soup or Marxism into your clothes. If, after forty years of communism, a person cannot have a glass of milk or a pair of shoes, he will not believe that communism is a good thing, no matter what you tell him."[30] However, optimistic hopes for a freer society were dashed in East Germany in 1953, Hungary in 1956, and in Czechoslovakia in 1968, when Soviet tanks were sent in to crush social protest movements or nationalist uprising.

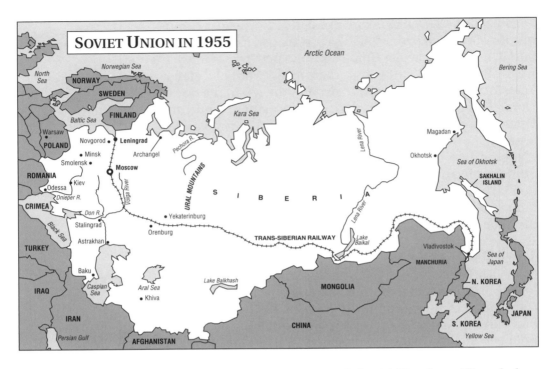

A serious crisis occurred in 1962 when Khrushchev shipped intercontinental missiles to Cuba, a communist nation in the Western Hemisphere. If installed, most of the United States would have been within reach of land-based Soviet rockets armed with nuclear warheads. President John F. Kennedy was ultimately successful in forcing Khrushchev to remove the missiles from Cuba, averting a possible nuclear war. But the making and handling of the crisis tarnished Khrushchev's reputation among members of the Soviet elite.

THE BREZHNEV PHASE

Although Khrushchev tried to introduce more democracy into the Communist Party, he left the totalitarian system intact. When he was on vacation in the Crimea in 1964, the Presidium (the body elected by the Supreme Soviet) voted him out of office and their decision was confirmed by the Central Committee the next day. Conservatives in the Politburo who had tried to rally against Khrushchev for years had finally succeeded. Thus Khrushchev was officially "retired," and he spent his final years in private life in Moscow. Not a single representative of the Soviet government attended his funeral in 1971.

By the late 1960s, the Soviet Union had achieved nuclear parity with the United States, although its GNP (gross national product) was still only half that of the United States. Soviet influence continued to expand in Africa, Central America, and Asia, a trend greeted with consternation in the West. The cold war competition led U.S. troops into two protracted wars, in Korea (1950–1953) and Vietnam (1964–1973). But East-West relations also began to improve in the 1970s, as witnessed by the numerous summits between Leonid Brezhnev, who replaced Khrushchev as general secretary of the Soviet Communist Party, and U.S. presidents Nixon, Ford, and Carter. Although the SALT (Strategic Arms Limitation Talks) meetings held in Helsinki, Finland, did not put an end to the arms race, they did help control the numbers of nuclear arms produced by both sides. Other talks on cooperation between

VOICES OF DISSENT

A broad community of dissenters who openly protested the Soviet regime began to develop in the 1960s, and by the 1970s many details of their mistreatment had been revealed to the outside world. The ruthless persecution of dissenters and their families included the practice of sending sane people to mental hospitals for horrific "rehabilitation" treatments. Some groups—Jews and Germans, for example—wanted the right to emigrate; others pleaded for religious freedom within the Soviet Union; all called for the protection of basic human rights.

Among the courageous voices of the dissenters, nuclear physicist Andrei Sakharov and his wife, Yelena Bonner, became well known in the West. Although awarded the Nobel Peace

Prize in 1975, Sakharov was refused a visa to Norway to accept the honor. In 1980, Sakharov was exiled to Gorki (as the Russian city Nizhni Novgorod was named from 1932 to 1991), a city forbidden to foreigners under the Soviets. He was unable to return to Moscow until Mikhail Gorbachev came to power.

Nobel Peace Prize laureate Andrei Sakharov personally suffered under the brutal Soviet regime.

nations and protection of basic human rights led to agreements known as the Helsinki Accords, signed in 1975 by thirty-five nations, including the Soviet Union and the United States.

The warming trend between the United States and the USSR was tested in 1979 when the Soviet Union invaded Afghanistan in support of its beleaguered communist government and against Muslim fighters who wanted to drive out both the Russians and communism. President Jimmy Carter feared Russian control of the Persian Gulf oil supplies and halted shipments of wheat and high-tech equipment from the United States to the Soviet Union. It took a decade for Russia to finally withdraw from Afghanistan, after suffering fifty thousand casualties. The fighting in Afghanistan continued between various ethnic and religious factions, without Russian involvement.

THE END OF THE OLD GUARD

By the 1980s, the growing technology gap between the USSR and Western companies and the stagnation of Russia's domestic economy and the bureaucratic machine that ran it put pressure on leaders for a change in direction. Yuri Andropov and then Konstantin Chernenko led Russia for short

U.S. president Jimmy Carter and Soviet prime minister Leonid Brezhnev sign the SALT II (Strategic Arms Limitation Talks) treaty in Vienna in 1979. Treaties such as these were signed in a climate of distrust and fear.

CHERNOBYL

The nuclear power plant explosion at Chernobyl in Ukraine on April 26, 1986, was a political as well as environmental catastrophe. Evidence of the disaster first appeared on a radiation detector in Sweden; residents of western Ukraine heard first reports over Polish radio. The Soviet government, despite glasnost, discredited itself by its initial response of withholding information and downplaying the scale of destruction. In fact, the incident was the worst such disaster to date.

The cost of cleanup and containment of the released radioactive material reaches into the billions of dollars. The final toll on the health of the exposed population (which includes 1.5 million Ukrainians, 10 percent of whom were severely irradiated by iodine-131) will not be known for years. Only one of Chernobyl's four original reactors is currently in use. Ukraine has agreed to shut down the last reactor by the year 2000, with the help of funds committed by the members of the G-7 group of industrialized nations.

periods, both dying in office after severe illnesses. When Mikhail Gorbachev was elected Party secretary in 1985, at the comparatively young age of fifty-four, he proposed a new program: perestroika (restructuring), glasnost (openness), and *demokratizatsiya* (democratization) were its bywords.

Many of Gorbachev's reforms struck at the heart of the communist system and led towards a free economy. "The market came with the dawn of civilization and it is not an invention of capitalism. . . . If it leads to improving the well-being of the people there is no contradiction with socialism,"[31] Gorbachev said. He proposed using profitability as a determining factor for an enterprise's survival—a departure from the policy of keeping a factory going, for instance, despite unprofitability, in order to ensure jobs. He sought to link workers' pay with their performance. He expanded opportunities for workers to become involved in management. He proposed a gradual shift from collective farms to individual control and ownership of the land. He permitted joint business ventures with foreign companies. Some people were in favor of these changes; others balked at losing subsidized prices, equal wages, and protection from unemployment.

Conservatives warned that these reforms would fail because the economy could not be half free and half controlled.

One of the most important consequences of Gorbachev's new, freer ways under glasnost was an increase of nationalism among non-Russian people in the Soviet Union. Secession became a prospect in the Baltic republics of Latvia, Estonia, and Lithuania. Ukraine, the second most populous republic (52 million) and an important center of agriculture and industry, also experienced a burst of nationalism. Other republics, such as Georgia, Moldavia, and Armenia, demanded more autonomy and sensitivity to ethnic and cultural issues. For the first time, the Soviet Union refrained from sending troops into Poland, Hungary, East Germany, Czechoslovakia, and Romania, despite the scope and speed of reforms that drove their communist governments out of office. Gorbachev also redefined the Soviet Union's Third World policy, shifting away from military expansionism and instead concentrating on political diplomacy and technological and economic cooperation.

THE COLLAPSE OF THE SOVIET UNION

By the spring of 1991 Russia was coping with instability at every turn. Difficulties in privatization contributed to a frustrating decline in the economy. Shortages of clothing and food staples contributed to a sharp rise in inflation. The budget deficit grew, and Soviet republic nations refused to make payments to the central government. Russia now had a parliament separate from the Supreme Soviet of the Soviet Union, and Boris Yeltsin, a new-thinking leader, became its popularly elected president. The communist monolith had faded away. Even President Yeltsin said, in 1990, "Let's not talk about Communism. Communism was just an idea, just pie in the sky."[32] In July 1991, Gorbachev asked the Soviet Communist Party to give up its Marxist ideology.

Hard-liners in the party leadership, those whose power was vested in the old order of state ownership and centralized planning, were appalled by this turn of events. A group from this faction attempted a coup in August 1991, isolating Gorbachev in the Crimea, where he was on vacation, and demanding control of the Soviet government and military. But the plotters met with massive resistance led by Yeltsin, who climbed aboard one of the tanks sent to surround the Rus-

Russians swarm around two tank drivers in Moscow during the coup of 1991. The crowds and much of the military present resisted the coup.

sian parliament buildings in Moscow and called on all citizens to resist the coup. Many sympathetic tank commanders turned their guns around to defend rather than attack government headquarters.

After the failure of the coup, Gorbachev returned to Moscow. He resigned as head of the Communist Party and banned its activities. Yeltsin met with the presidents of Ukraine and Byelorussia (Belarus) and formed the Commonwealth of Independent States (CIS), with no ties to the former Soviet government. Most of the other former Soviet republics joined the CIS, with the exception of the Baltic states, which had already gone their own way, and Georgia (which did join the CIS in 1994). On December 25, 1991, the Soviet Union ceased to exist. Across Russia the Soviet hammer and sickle flag was replaced by the three-colored Russian flag, dating from Peter the Great's time.

4

THE NEW RUSSIA

The Russian Federation is not as vast as the old Soviet Union, but at 6.6 million square miles it is still the largest state in the world. The Russian Federation includes twenty-one autonomous republics, forty-nine provinces (oblasts), six territories *(krai)*, and ten national districts *(okrugs)*.

A VARIED POPULATION

Almost twice the land area of the United States, the Russian Federation contains a population of 148 million people. More than 80 percent of the people are ethnic Russians, compared with 51 percent at the last full census of the Soviet Union in 1989. More than three-quarters of the people live in urban areas, leaving three-quarters of the land thinly populated or virtually uninhabited. The three regions of Russia where Russians are not the majority are in the Ural Mountains, where inhabitants are of Turkic and Finnic descent, the ancestors of the khanate of Khazan; on the slopes of the Caucasus, where a mosaic of ethnic groups, including Georgians, Avars, Chechens, and others, predominates; and across eastern Siberia, populated by Yakut, Buryat, and Tuvinian peoples.

The ethnic checkerboard of the mountainous Caucasus region has a vivid and complex history. Rivalries continue to shape the future of the region. For example, after the collapse of the Soviet Union, Chechnya, a republic of the Russian Federation in the northern Caucasus, declared its independence. At least 95 percent of ethnic Chechens are Sunni Muslims and have been struggling with Russia on and off for hundreds of years. After three years of tolerating Chechen independence, in 1994 Russian troops invaded to try to force Chechnya back into the federation. In the bloody conflict that followed, one hundred thousand people lost their lives, and huge areas of the capital, Grozny, were destroyed, as well as towns, villages, and countryside. Finally, Russian troops withdrew and a truce was signed in 1996, which put off finalizing the political status of Chechnya until 2001.

The present Russian government must also be concerned for the interests of Russians outside of Russia proper. Some 25.3 million Russians live beyond the borders of the Russian Federation. Almost a quarter of the population of Ukraine is Russian (11.4 million of 37.4 million), 7.1 million Russians live in Kazakhstan and Kyrgyzstan, and another 3.2 million Russians live in Belarus, Latvia, Estonia, and Moldova. Russian is the language spoken by 90 percent of the people across the Russian Federation, whatever their ethnic origin. Ukrainian and Belorussian, however, are the official languages of independent Ukraine and Belarus.

A NEW ECONOMY

Russia's transition from communism to a market economy has required a tremendous transformation of society, requiring new forms of financing, management, regulation, and legal protection. Formerly, the state had owned virtually everything—all the assets of the country. Beginning in 1992, Russia embarked on privatization, the transferring of these assets to the private sector.

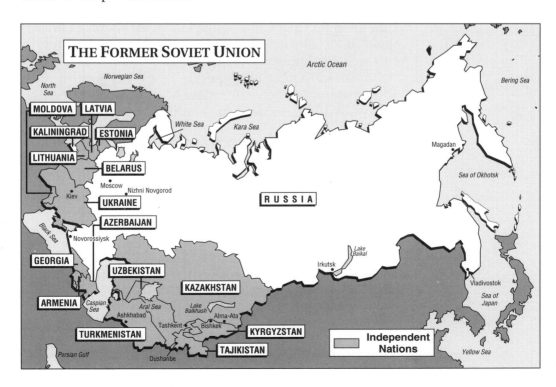

A decree freeing prices took effect in the beginning of 1992. The expected inflation was brutal as prices on many goods, including staples such as food and clothing, soared to unheard-of levels. The relative value of the currency dropped precipitously. In 1988 one ruble was worth $1.59. In 1997, one ruble was worth $.000176, or, in different terms, $1.00 was worth 5,683 rubles. The impact of inflation was overwhelming for many people, especially for the elderly, the disabled, and students. However, the market mechanisms of supply and demand kept goods in the stores, and the long lines that had been the hallmark of daily life under the Soviet system (Soviet women typically had spent fifteen hours a week in lines) quickly disappeared. Inflation leveled off at an annual rate of about 20 percent by 1997.

The framework of privatization called for distributing vouchers to all 150 million Russian citizens, which could then be used to buy shares in state-owned enterprises. In a typical firm, managers and workers received 51 percent of ownership, with the rest in the public voucher system. Local agencies carried out voucher auctions. However, most people did not use their vouchers to buy shares directly. They sold them for cash or exchanged them for shares in investment funds. The intermediaries then used the vouchers to buy shares in enterprises.

Privatization proceeded quickly. By 1994 majority ownership in about 120,000 enterprises was transferred from the government to private owners. Massive public education

THE RUSSIAN BABEL

There are 175 languages in existence in Russia, a dozen or so of which are close to extinction. Those endangered include Vod, a Baltic tongue; Yugh, spoken in western Siberia; Kerek, from the Kamchatka Peninsula; and Aleut, a language of the far north. These and other tongues have been adversely affected by the collapse of state aid to remote villages.

Some ethnic republics have seen a resurgence of interest in national languages in the way they are both written and spoken. Latin script is being reintroduced for Tatar in Tatarstan (the switch to Cyrillic script was made in 1939 under Stalin). And a group in Buryatia, in southeast Siberia, is studying the restoration of Old Mongol lettering for Buryat.

campaigns supported the process and resulted in fully 98 percent of the population picking up their vouchers.

Although much progress has been made, complex obstacles to a successful reorganization of Russia's economy remain unsolved. At first, Russia's industrial output fell dramatically. New enterprises lacked capital resources. Management was in disarray. Supply and sales networks were disrupted. And the government failed to provide a climate which could give confidence to business—that is, to collect taxes, to provide a legal framework to enforce contracts, to protect against corruption, and to maintain the value of the currency.

Soviet citizens wait in line to purchase groceries in 1990. Although economic reforms benefited some, Russia is still plagued with food shortages.

TWO SETS OF BOOKS

Overall, the economy is more stable today, but it is difficult to describe it with any reliability. Official statistics still paint a bleak picture, with a GNP (gross national product) declining for six consecutive years (1990 to 1996). There has been a corresponding statistical decline in the standard of living and a rise in unemployment. The payment of wages and pensions was more than $10 billion behind in 1997 for millions of factory workers, farmers, doctors, firefighters, police, miners,

THE ENVIRONMENT

Some 15 percent of the territory of Russia is classified as ecological disaster areas. Unrecorded hazardous waste has been dumped throughout the country and groundwater has been subsequently contaminated. Radiation "hot spots" from sites of underground nuclear explosions as well as from small-scale use of radioactive materials render large areas uninhabitable. Routine leakage of oil and oil products from Russia's pipeline network is 5 million tons a year; across Siberia there are lakes of spilled oil. Air pollution from car and truck traffic is on the rise, although levels of factory-produced air pollution have declined.

Also, Siberian forests are in danger of disappearing. By law, 2 million hectares a year are supposed to be replanted, but a further 9 million hectares a year are felled illegally and not replanted. At the present rate, the forests will disappear within thirty years. The leadership of the Russian Federation must confront these very serious problems to safeguard Russia's still vast natural resources for future generations.

engineers, scientists, schoolteachers, and retirees. However, a 1995 survey revealed that 40 percent of family incomes was not being reported to tax and statistics collectors, meaning that purchasing power was actually 67 percent higher than officially reported. "Most Russians have been experiencing an improved standard of living since 1994," [33] according to Avraham Shama, a professor at the University of New Mexico who has just completed a study of the Russian economy. While collecting data for his study, Shama heard many stories like this one, as told by one businessman who owns three book, magazine, and newspaper kiosks: "My sales are up by 10 to 20 percent per month, and so are profits. I invest 90 percent of my profit in expanding my business. . . . I declare only 10 percent of my revenues and profits [as taxable income]. . . . If I declare all my profit, I will have to pay most of it as taxes." [34]

The common permissive attitude towards tax evasion and other accounting indiscretions is perpetuated by the fact that the government does not live up to its basic promises, such as paying timely wages to state workers and military personnel and pensions to retired people. Commenting on petty thievery in the workplace, one Russian government official said,

"One factor pushing people into this is that if a worker hasn't been paid for three months and he knows that a stolen component can be sold for such-and-such a price, and he takes it, then what you have is a state at war with its workers."[35] Few people are unsympathetic to workers in these circumstances.

However, the blurring of the distinction between legal and illegal activity takes on a different cast when it comes to the blackmail, intimidation, and racketeering of the Russian mafia. The slaying of an American businessman, Paul Tatum, in Moscow in 1996 in an apparent contract murder shocked the foreign business community. The new crime bosses use KGB-trained (the KGB was the former Soviet Union's secret police–intelligence agency) assassins and techniques; Tatum was killed by automatic weapon fire on a Sunday afternoon at a metro station in central Moscow. "Russia is a bubbling cauldron of criminal organizations—Sicily [home of the infamous Sicilian mafia] on a giant scale,"[36] proclaimed a recent article in *Forbes* magazine. Corruption mushrooms into the realm of politics when wealthy gangsters contribute to political campaigns, and then elected leaders owe them favors and protection, a "roof," as it is called in Russian slang.

American businessman Paul Tatum was gunned down by Russian gangsters in a Moscow subway station on November 3, 1996. Tatum built the Western-style Radisson-Slavyanskaya hotel that stands behind him.

FOREIGN INVESTMENT

Although crime and corruption have scared some potential investors away, Russia is still attracting foreign investment and joint venture enterprises. Western firms are pouring resources into Russia, seeking a stake in profits to be made. One American investment firm commented, "The quality of companies is much better in Russia than in other Eastern European countries."[37] By 1997, private investors in the United States and other countries held more than $1.4 billion in Russian assets. At least four Russian stocks were scheduled to be listed on the New York Stock Exchange in 1997, with several dozen expected in the next five years.

Other investments are made directly between corporations. For example, a paper plant in Nizhni Novgorod, Russia's third-largest city (which has had a successful privatization in general), won a $150 million foreign investment from a German paper company. The company is now 90 percent owned by foreigners, and the forty-eight hundred workers are being paid three times the going rate. The World Bank's International Finance Corporation has played a role in structuring many of these transactions, and it has also bolstered investor confidence in Russia by including it for the first time in 1996 in their widely watched index of emerging markets.

The International Monetary Fund (IMF), an important international financial institution, has a $10.1 billion, three-year loan in place to Russia. To receive the money, Russia has had to live up to agreements concerning the government's fiscal responsibility. Loan payments to Russia have been suspended by the IMF several times because of the Russian government's chronic inability to collect taxes from its citizens and corporations so that in turn the government can pay its bills and meet its obligations. However, each of these setbacks has been temporary.

Political progress toward participatory democracy has helped Russia secure these international loans and aid. Multiple political parties are beginning to build constituencies on the basis of issues, not just personalities. The Duma elections of 1995 and the presidential election of 1996 were important milestones. Over 70 percent of the voters cast ballots

In front of their home, two elderly women cast their ballots in the 1996 government elections. The elections drew over 70 percent of the voters.

in the first round of the presidential election compared with 49 percent of registered voters in the U.S. presidential election of the same year. Independent news coverage has had a major impact on the quality of information available preceding elections and on important, ongoing issues. For the first time, city governments are developing budgets, publishing them, and holding public hearings. And the establishment of a new Russian Civil Code in 1996 offers further protection for contracts and business transactions.

NEW WEALTH AND AFFLUENCE

Critics of Russian privatization point to the accumulation of massive wealth by a handful of people, insiders who obtained major shareholdings at bargain prices. Speculation in land, real estate, and currency also created quick fortunes for those connected to insider circles of power. Dissenters resented the transformation of political influence into personal wealth.

Others made fortunes legally, such as real estate investors with cash to buy up newly privatized apartment buildings, refurbish them, and resell them at handsome profits. Banking has been very profitable and has become an elite profession in Russia. Management, marketing, and finance skills are also at a premium in newly restructured industries.

Small business is growing: Labor surveys show that employment in small businesses grew from 6.5 million in 1994 to 8.8 million in 1995, producing 12 percent of all goods in Russia in that year. These small firms, however, account for only 9 percent of Russian employment, compared with 37 percent in the Czech Republic and 23 percent in Poland. Some experts say that the small percentage shows how much room there is for growth in this sector.

City dwellers have benefited more from the new economy than rural folk, and Moscow's residents have gained most of all. All but one of the country's top twenty-five banks are in Moscow, and 80 percent of all the country's deposits are said to be lodged in them. Moscow's living standards were higher than the rest of the country's during the Soviet era, too, but today Moscow's boom economy is creating a new divide. For example, Ford Motor Company says that nearly half of all Russians who can afford its cars live in Moscow. Moscow's residents are twice as likely as other urban Russians to have traveled abroad. They are also more than twice as likely to own a telephone, personal computer, microwave oven, or credit card. Unemployment and late wages are less often a problem in Moscow than elsewhere.

LOSING GROUND

In contrast to Moscow, many other areas have not lived up to initial hopes for an economic rejuvenation. In general, smaller Russian cities that depend heavily on specialized industries have been crippled by the initial decrease in industrial output. For instance, the economy of Vladivostok, Russia's gateway to the Pacific in the Far East region, was heavily tied to military bases, weapons plants, and the port facilities that housed Russia's Pacific Fleet. The fleet is now less than half its former size—about fifteen hundred ships have been scrapped and thousands of sailors have left the area. Currently, the region is characterized by budget cuts and strikes. There are also frequent blackouts, as the cash-starved power companies cannot provide dependable electricity, leaving thousands of people in towns and villages in cold and dark living quarters.

Throughout Russia, pensioners have seen their incomes and savings shrink due to inflation. Until recently, many older people could be seen in Moscow congregating at Tishinka, a cheap outdoor flea market, selling their threadbare possessions in an effort to survive. Police closed the flea market in 1996, making way for the construction of a new mall. Children have also suffered in the new system, especially children in large low-income or single-parent families. As many as 4 million people in Russia are homeless, according to a report prepared for the British Charities Aid Foundation. There are few shelters, and many homeless people live in train stations, parks, and underpasses. Estimates of homeless children range from three hundred thousand to 1 million.

SCIENCE FAILS IN THE NEW ECONOMY

The collapse of Soviet science has been another sad consequence of the end of the Soviet system. Russian and American policy makers have focused on preserving "big science," meaning space, nuclear weapons, and military research and development. Unfortunately, this has left the majority of researchers in other fields without support.

Young homeless children in Moscow form a line to receive hot soup. In spite of reforms, as many as 1 million children may be homeless in Russia.

Many research institutes were still not paying regular salaries in 1997 and could not fund research. For example, the Russian Academy of Sciences, which had a $288 million budget in the 1980s and led dozens of international expeditions, had only a $36 million annual budget in 1996. The Institute of Theoretical and Experimental Physics (ITEP) in Moscow is another case in point. In addition to its research functions, this institute is one of a few that also trains top high school physics graduates. But many of ITEP's experimental physics projects have ground to a halt. Short on cash for electricity, the institute was forced to shut down its ten-gigaelectron-volt accelerator.

In science, the legacy of separation of research from teaching in the Soviet system has been a major obstacle to recovery. Most universities only employ a small handful of scientists with sufficient expertise to lecture on current trends in their fields. Promising graduate students see few viable science careers. One source of Western help has been the International Soros Science Education Program, launched by international investor George Soros in 1994. The program has helped fund positions for professors and high school science teachers as well as undergraduate and graduate study, allocating $135 million to Russia over a three-year period.

EXPANDING HOUSING

What many Russians want more than anything else is an improvement in their living conditions. Under the Soviet

EATING WELL, RUSSIAN STYLE

The center of the Russian home is the table, which for a traditional meal would be laden with an assortment of *zakuski*, or appetizers. These may include salads dressed in sour cream; pickled tomatoes and marinated mushrooms; sardines, mackerel, herring, or sturgeon in various sauces; vegetable caviars; and piping hot *pirozhki* (meat or vegetable pies), all with horseradish on the side and a choice of rye or white bread. Next comes the main course of meat or poultry, perhaps cooked with fruit and accompanied by potatoes or rice. Dessert might be an assortment of pies, cakes, sweet breads, and chocolates, served with Russian tea and followed by cognac or a treasured liqueur. The entire meal is usually served with vodka or wine.

Most Russian homes have small refrigerators and little storage space, so most Russians go to the market every day. Bread is a daily purchase and, in most families, it never lasts long enough to go stale.

system, the state guaranteed housing to all citizens, and rents were low. But the Soviet regime often failed to live up to its guarantee, and there were long waiting lists in the cities for adequate living quarters. Furthermore, the high-rise apartment buildings built under the Soviet system were frequently criticized: Living spaces were exceedingly cramped, hallways and public areas were poorly kept, and the monotonous, barracklike buildings were an eyesore that made most cities look alike. A family of four would typically occupy a four-room apartment consisting of a children's bedroom, a combination living/dining/bedroom for the parents, and a small kitchen and bathroom. After 1962 some Russians could purchase apartments in cooperative housing units, which could offer more living space per person. Others lived in communal housing, where as many as ten to eighteen families share a building with one kitchen and several public bathrooms.

New efforts are under way to create more choice and expand home ownership. Developers are trying out single-family and low-rise, lower-density housing. But a major obstacle is the lack of a home mortgage system in the Russian banking industry. Buyers today usually must have the cash or be satisfied with a short-term (three-year) loan at a high interest rate.

DACHAS AND COUNTRY LIFE

For many urban Russians, the apartment is just a place to eat and sleep during the week; they pour their energy into their dachas (country cottages) outside the cities, where they spend weekends from April to September and grow vegetables in garden plots. Recent surveys indicate that more than half of Russia's population has some access to a dacha. Retired people stay for the whole summer, sometimes with their grandchildren. The dachas have helped many people put food on the table: In 1993, for example, an astonishing 83 percent of all potatoes grown were produced on private plots. In the same year, 36 percent of all agricultural production came from these private plots, which represent less than 3 percent of all agricultural land. Produce from the garden is carefully harvested, with the excess stored in root cellars, pickled, and preserved. Until 1991 the size of the dacha was strictly limited by the government—no more than 720 square yards for the garden and no more than 30 square yards for the building (plus an additional 12 square yards for a patio). Today, these restrictions have been lifted, and the attractive results can be seen in the countryside.

In rural areas, private ownership of housing is more common, but living conditions remain primitive. "Within a few minutes from Moscow along the main road to St. Petersburg you will see women hand-pumping water from the well and carrying it home," report Richard Layard and John Parker in *The Coming Russian Boom.* "In the whole country, nearly half of rural homes are without water and over half without sewerage."[38] Most of Russia's farms have gone on as undercapitalized and inefficient operations, although two-thirds are now in private partnerships, joint stock companies, or cooperatives. Agricultural production was still in decline in 1997, and thousands of farms have folded. Change may be coming, but it will take long to improve the circumstances of rural people.

IN SCHOOLS

One of Russia's achievements is its literacy rate: About 98 percent of Russians can read. Traditionally, Russian education

With the portraits of the late Nicholas II and his wife watching from above, young Russian cadets play in their military high school. The number of private schools in Russia is increasing.

has been strong in mathematics and the physical sciences. In a recent test of thirteen-year-olds given in forty-one countries, Russian students scored higher than U.S. students in both math and science.

Since 1991, some teachers have clung to the old Communist textbooks and rote methods of learning, while others are inspired to use once-banned books and new teaching methods. But many good teachers are leaving state schools and turning to the business sector or newly created private schools, where they can earn more money. Private schools also offer a wider curriculum than that found in state schools. Even religious schools, illegal since 1917, are beginning to reappear.

School begins on the first day of September for most Russian children, from the age of six (first grade) until they have completed the eleventh grade, although only nine grades are mandatory. Primary schools of four years are followed by middle schools, beginning at age ten. After middle school, students choose between several types of senior high schools. Some high schools offer vocational or technical training, and graduates prepare to work in skilled or semiskilled jobs in industry, agriculture, or offices. Other schools prepare students for study in the universities. Outside of this pattern of schooling, special schools exist to develop special proficiencies and talents in economics, mathematics, art, ballet, or foreign languages.

To be admitted to the university, secondary school graduates must pass both a written and an oral exam. Russian students generally apply for study in a chosen field at one university only. Competition is notoriously stiff. Should a student fail to be admitted, he or she might work and slowly complete a degree in an evening study program. University studies last four to six years and include the completion of a thesis before graduation. Advanced graduate degrees are more difficult to obtain than their American counterparts, since they require major original contributions to one's specialized field.

Because of the high inflation of the last few years, state spending on education has actually fallen. Most university departments have barely enough funds to pay small salaries to their staffs. Russian intellectuals, such as writer and former dissident Aleksandr Solzhenitsyn, have spoken out against neglecting education and science. "There is a terrifying split in society. . . . We are in great danger now," Solzhenitsyn said. "Our schools [and] science are rotting away."[39]

MEDICAL CARE

The stated goal of the Soviet health care system was to provide the entire population with free, high-quality medical care. Unfortunately, health care in Russia has been of mediocre quality, suffering from the Soviet contempt for doctors (they are in the so-called nonproductive sector of the economy) and lack of adequate medical equipment and supplies. Russia has an oversupply of physicians, the majority of whom are women, poorly paid and inadequately trained. Factory workers earn twice the average salary of doctors. Russians sometimes refuse medical care because of lack of confidence in the system. Bribery and backdoor payments to doctors is often the only way to get better care; doctors are forced to accept such payments in order to support themselves and their own families.

Problems in health and medical care have contributed to a declining life expectancy for Russian citizens. By the end of 1993, male life expectancy had fallen to fifty-nine years, and in 1997, to fifty-eight, the lowest of any industrialized nation. Infant mortality is high: Twenty-six infants per one thousand die per year before the age of one. More people are dying each year in Russia than are born, thus Russian statistics put the growth rate at -0.07 percent. Leading causes of death are cardiovascular disease and cancer, but infectious and communicable diseases such as diphtheria and tuberculosis are on the rise because of inadequate immunization coverage and a severe shortage of medical resources. AIDS and other sexually transmitted diseases are also on the rise due to soaring narcotic abuse and the lack of educational or preventive measures available.

The nutrition and health consciousness of Americans has not spread to Russia. The traditional Russian diet is high in fat and cholesterol, and alcoholism, smoking, lack of exercise, and stress pose serious health risks.

FAMILIES

About 90 percent of Russians live within a family. Traditionally, the extended family lived together, including grandparents, parents, and children, especially in rural areas. Now, three generations live under one roof in 20 percent of Russian families.

Russians treasure their families and close friends. The closeness and hospitality of Russian families, typically described in nineteenth-century classic Russian literature, endures in the twentieth century. Reliance on one's trusted circle was especially important during the Stalin era, when denunciations could ruin a person's livelihood and endanger personal well-being.

The divorce rate in Russia is about 30 percent and has tripled since 1960, so it is not uncommon for Russians to marry twice or more. Marriage is legal at age eighteen, but most Russians marry in their twenties. After the official ceremony, newlyweds frequently visit historic sites, where they leave flowers, and then celebrate with a wedding feast, replete with toasts, music, and singing.

Most Russian women work outside the home. While women's rights are protected by law, women still predominate in low-paid jobs, and only a handful rise to top decision-making positions. Employment ads soliciting workers on the basis of their sex or age (prohibited in the United States as a violation of the 1964 Civil Rights Act) are the norm in Russia, where gender and age discrimination cases are not brought to court. A bright light for women are new opportunities in small businesses; for instance, by early 1997 women had received nearly half of the loans to Russia made so far by a $300 million revolving fund of the European Bank for Reconstruction and Development.

The social life of young people used to revolve around organized Communist groups, such as the Octobrists, for ages six to nine, the Pioneers, for ages ten to fifteen, and then the Komsomols, for ages fourteen to twenty-eight. These organizations were disbanded in 1991. Today, group activities are still the norm for young people, but they are more likely to be school-based extracurricular activities or informal outings to films, parties, or a park.

Soviet society prided itself on protecting children from the need to work; only adults were allowed to take any sort of job.

But today, these rules have relaxed, and enterprising teen-agers can be found washing cars, filling office odd jobs, or posting ads on city walls.

SPORTS

Sports competition became a powerful propaganda tool in the days of the cold war, and the Soviet state put a premium on the development of Olympic champions. Since 1991, the new leadership has sought to reform Russian sports, separating elite programs from mass-participation sports for the first time. Well-known sports stars took part in attacking the old Soviet system, including the world chess champion, Gary Kasparov, and Yuri Vlasov, a former Olympic weight-lifting champion, who campaigned against the KGB in the Russian parliament. Currently, two-thirds of sports financing comes from local budgets, while the state supports regional sports committees. The Russian Olympic Committee is supported by the state but also is allowed to earn money on its own. Thus it has signed contracts with major world producers of sports equipment, as have clubs and federations further down the sports hierarchy.

A boy playfully splashes water on his sister as his family washes a carpet. Russian families are particularly close-knit and some include three generations living together.

The most popular sports in Russia are soccer and ice hockey. Children are encouraged to try out a wide range of athletic activity, including cross-country skiing, gymnastics, track, swimming, volleyball, tennis, and other team sports. There is still a great interest in Olympic winners in Russia, but the attitude is different. "It's first and foremost a great festival, a game," [40] said Irina Privalova, Russia's famous sprinter, in *Russian Life* magazine, summing up the new spirit.

THE CULTURAL HORIZON

Despite the chaos and uncertainty that characterizes many aspects of living in Russia, the explosive energy of this newly opened society is what visitors find most remarkable. The influx of Western cultural imports such as rock and roll music, MTV, and fast food restaurants is also impacting the lives of Russians—especially Russian youth. Just how these forces will ultimately shape the lives and attitudes of a new generation of Russians is yet to be seen.

ARTS AND TRADITIONS: BINDING OLD AND NEW

The Russian Federation's new spirit can most easily be observed in the cultural life of its cities, which, beginning with perestroika in 1985, have become vibrant centers of activity. After years of censorship of the arts, what was once forbidden is now read and seen and listened to. There is new popular music in the nightclubs and on the radio; there are new restaurants everywhere, new art in the galleries, and a myriad of books in the bookstores. Museums, concert halls, theaters, and exhibitions have a full range of offerings to suit audiences' and patrons' varied interests. Moscow and St. Petersburg are the most important cultural centers, attracting artists, musicians, and writers from smaller cities and faraway provinces.

RELIGIOUS REVIVAL AND CHURCH RENOVATION

Although a flood of international influences and the free flow of information have galvanized artistic creation, Russia is also experiencing a revival of interest in its own historical and cultural roots. This includes the gradual rehabilitation and rebuilding of Russia's churches, most of which were closed or used for nonreligious purposes under communism. In 1917, Russia had around 45,000 functioning churches. By 1939, barely 100 remained in use. Many Russians still remember Stalin's 1931 order for the destruction of the largest and most richly decorated church in Russia, the Church of Christ the Savior near Moscow's Kremlin. Countless religious paintings, 48 marble reliefs, and 177 marble tablets were demolished, and each of its five domes, including the 335-foot-high central dome, were blown up. Stalin planned to erect a Palace of Soviets in its place; it was never built. In a remarkable turnaround, a film recording the destruction of the Church of Christ the Savior was shown for the first time publicly in 1988, the one thousandth anniversary of Russia's official conversion to Christianity in 988. In 1991 Russia's new leadership warmly embraced the Russian Orthodox Church.

The churches themselves, with their intricate, variegated forms, provide a unique and symbolic contrast to the monotonous, concrete structures built under communism. Although the masonry churches of Byzantium influenced the building and design of Russia's first churches (which were wooden), church architecture in Russia developed its own unique styles. The simplest, rectangular edifices made from wood were enlarged to become octagons, covered by a roof with eight slopes. This form, a striking invention of the Russians, became known as the "tented" church.

Masonry churches were preferred by the princes and tsars, both for aesthetic reasons and for protection against fire, which ravaged Moscow and other cities innumerable times. In the twelfth century, a Russian version of Byzantine forms developed, including the distinctive Russian "onion" dome, the Church of St. Nicholas in Novgorod (1113) being an early example. Another rich melding of styles occurred when Renaissance forms were assimilated and blended with native elements in the fifteenth and sixteenth centuries. The seventeenth century produced a profusion of lavishly ornamented churches and monasteries.

The most magnificent surviving wooden church in Russia is the Church of the Transfiguration (1714) on the island of Kizhi in Lake Onega in northern Russia. It has a core of three octagons and four rectangular compartments in a cruciform, or cross-shaped, design. The intricate roofing, from which rise twenty-two cupolas, or domelike structures, lends it a festive, fairy-tale appearance. Other wooden churches survive, some of which have been moved to a museum near the city of Archangel. At the Open Air Wooden Architecture Museum, about ninety historic churches and other wooden buildings can be toured in a beautifully wooded setting. The museum also sponsors concerts of folk music and dancing and studios for craftsmen producing traditional folk art.

OTHER RELIGIONS REEMERGE

Other religious groups suffered under communism, and they are also experiencing a revival today. The Jewish religious community and ethnic Jews in general came under sus-

Ornate wood shingles decorate the domes of the Church of the Transfiguration in Russia. The gables are said to resemble the tall headdresses worn by women in medieval Russia.

tained pressure from the Soviet state, in part driven by continued anti-Semitism. Only sixty synagogues remained in the Soviet Union in the 1980s, reduced from more than a thousand in 1917; half of these remaining synagogues were in Transcaucasia and Central Asia, where only a fraction of Soviet Jews lived. Under perestroika, a religious revival began to take place among Russians with Jewish backgrounds, and lively contacts developed with Jewish communities abroad. Today, many synagogues have been returned to worshipers, and Jewish educational establishments are spreading.

At the time of the 1917 revolution there were several hundred thousand Buddhists among the Mongol peoples in Buryatia (in Siberia) and Kalmykia (on the Caspian Sea, south of the Volga River). Buddhist institutions were destroyed in the late 1930s. In the 1990s, Buddhist monasteries were reestablished in these republics within the Russian Federation.

ICONS, FROM OLD TO NEW

As old churches are being reopened and celebrated, the frescoes and icons (religious paintings) they contain are receiving the attention they were long denied. Many thousands of these works of art were hidden in basements for decades, after the churches they were rescued from were destroyed. Slowly, the number of works recovered, restored, and exhibited increases.

Icon painting in particular has a long and meaningful history. From the tenth to the end of the seventeenth century, all painting in Russia revolved around the production of icons. An artistic code laid down by the church dictated many aspects of their creation. The paintings had to avoid any suggestion of statuary, which was forbidden by the church, and therefore painters could not use perspective as a technique.

UNDERSTANDING ICONS

Icons were frequently painted on wood panels covered with *levkas,* a mixture of chalk, linen, oil, and glue made of sturgeon bones and skin. Halos and backgrounds in gold leaf added richness and brilliance, and a protective coat of boiled linseed oil gave an overall golden tone to the painting. (The earliest surviving icons, from the late tenth to the twelfth centuries of Kievan Rus, include frescoes and mosaics.) Interestingly, the only source of light is from within the saint, which was intended to depict "the uncreated light of God," as an art historian explains in *The Cambridge Encyclopedia of Russia.*

Typically, a number of icons were assembled in the church in a high screen between the altar and the sanctuary. This screen became known as the iconostasis, the symbolic barrier and borderline between two worlds, the eternal and the temporal. In Moscow's churches, by the fifteenth century the iconostases were multitiered, each tier containing a specified grouping of icons, with definite positions assigned to certain subjects. The assemblage became a tool of instruction for the frequently illiterate congregation, "the Bible for the masses," as writer Arthur Voyce noted in his book *Moscow and the Roots of Russian Culture.*

Icons were not only found in churches. In private homes, icons were often placed in every room, at the head of each bed, even hung on barns and stables to guard the livestock. Other icons were set up at crossroads for travelers; still others were carried in religious and imperial processions and into battle.

But within this strict, two-dimensional tradition, icons spanned a variety of styles and moods; some were masterpieces.

Icons were unsigned: The name one might see is the name of the saint depicted. However, icon painter and monk Andrei Rublev (1360–1430) became known during his lifetime, and after his death he acquired an even greater reputation. Many existing icons are attributed to Rublev, but the most famous is the Old Testament Trinity of 1411, which hangs in the Tretyakov Gallery in Moscow. Its subject is the visit of three angels to Abraham and Sarah, and it is renowned for its graceful composition, harmony of color, and dreamy mood.

In the last ten years, the tradition of icon painting has also begun a slow revival. There are icon workshops in all major monasteries, most notably in Sergiyev Posad outside Moscow, in Optina Pustyn near Kaluga, and in Novgorod's St. George's Monastery. These workshops preserve the old techniques. "After I started painting icons, my outlook on the world changed," said a professional icon painter in *Russian Life* magazine. "The painter has to feel the icon with his heart and soul." Another icon painter commented: "We are connected to our ancestors through icons. If the traditions are preserved, then the culture and the people will flourish and develop in the future."[41]

Rublev's Old Testament Trinity icon depicts three angels. From the tenth to the end of the seventeenth century, all Russian painting focused on the production of icons.

SECULAR ART

The number one tourist attraction of the Russian Federation for Russians and foreign visitors alike is the State Hermitage Museum in St. Petersburg, which is housed in three buildings: the Winter Palace (the home of the imperial family until 1917), the Small Hermitage, and the Large Hermitage. The museum's holdings are vast; particularly famous are its collections of Russian history, prehistoric times (including Scythian relics), Byzantium, the art of Central Asia, Western art, and oriental and classical antiquities. The buildings themselves are of great interest, with their remarkable interiors and features.

Secular art had its beginnings in Russia under Peter the Great, when an important school of Russian painting emerged. Foreign artists were employed at the Russian court in St. Petersburg, and Russian artists were sent abroad to study painting in the studios of Paris, Amsterdam, Antwerp, and Florence. The Imperial Academy of Arts, founded in 1757 in St. Petersburg, strove to establish a European standard of cosmopolitanism.

From Peter's group of "fledgling" painters emerged three fine artists, Ivan Nikitin (1690–1741), Alexei Antropov (1716–1795), and Andrei Matveyev (1701–1739). Perhaps because of the influence of icon painting, the Russian artists excelled at painting portraits. "In their portraits, they tried to show not only the physical likenesses but the souls of their subjects, without glossing over any of their less attractive characteristics," [42] writes cultural historian Suzanne Massie. The

Vladimir Borovikovsky's painting of Catherine II taking a stroll in the park is considered important for its candid, informal portrayal.

great portrait artists of Catherine the Great's time were Dmitry Levitsky (1735–1822) and Vladimir Borovikovsky (1757–1825). Borovikovsky's portrait of the aging Catherine walking her dog in a park was unusually informal and candid, greatly influencing later portraits of royalty. Ivan Argunov (1727–1802) and Mikhail Shibanov (died after 1789) became known for their portraits of Russian peasants, for the first time preserving glimpses of peasant weddings and other celebrations.

By the nineteenth century, Russian art progressed in tandem with the European Classical, Romantic, and Realistic mainstream movements. One of the first Russian painters to earn an international reputation was Karl Briullov (1798–1877), a member of the Academies of Bologna, Milan, Parma, and Florence and the recipient of an important honor in Paris. Aside from his fine portraits, Briullov also took on historical and mythological subjects, one of the grand trends of nineteenth-century painting.

Two other portraitists, Orest Kiprensky (1782–1836) and Vasily Tropinin (1776–1857) were both sons of serfs. While Kiprensky produced many fine paintings of aristocrats, treasured for their thoughtful and refined energy, Tropinin chose ordinary people for his subjects and painted them with a sympathetic interest. Following Tropinin, Alexei Venetsianov (1780–1847) recorded the quiet and unchanging life of Russia's peasants, in scenes directly and carefully observed. By the mid–nineteenth century, artists were taking on topics like the inequality of women and the impoverishment of the aristocracy.

ART IN THE TWENTIETH CENTURY

Russian realism of the late nineteenth century gave way to the explosion of modernism and its branch movements in the early twentieth century, with a generation of brilliant artists including Vasily Kandinsky (1866–1944), Mikhail Vrubel (1856–1910), Kasimir Malevich (1878–1935), and Marc Chagall (1887–1985).

Beginning in the 1930s and continuing more or less until the late 1980s, Soviet art developed in isolation, subject to political pressures and the caprices of individual "culture tsars." There was a painful distinction between "soviet" art and "contemporary" art, distinguishing between state-sponsored art and art made outside of official channels. Today, that gap

SOCIALIST REALISM

After a period of building pressure in the 1920s against artists of the avant-garde, or experimental vanguard, the Communist government in 1932 abolished alternative movements to socialist realism, the approved style. Based on the presumption that art could elevate and even transform society, socialist realism guided painting, architecture, and the performing arts. "Realism" really meant "idealism." All permitted art had to adhere to Marxist-Leninist philosophy and support the goals of the Communist Party. The movement was anonymously defined as "a method of praising our leaders in a way even they will understand."

Socialist realism took its most noteworthy form in the production of vast quantities of posters with simple, bold images intended to elevate and instruct the common people. In the 1920s, poster artists turned from revolutionary slogans to public health and education issues. In the 1930s, posters embraced industrialization. During World War II, posters dealt with foreign policy topics and defense. Although television probably weakened the power of the posters' messages, the medium was revived at the end of the communist era. In the 1980s, posters were used to expose the corrupt bureaucracy and draw attention to Stalinist crimes.

has closed, and Russian artists are again part of an international dialogue. Cultural exchange programs with foreign countries, international exhibitions, symposia on contemporary art, training programs for curators and arts management, fellowships for artists, and media coverage of these activities are the norm now in Russia.

Most contemporary galleries are in Moscow; few private galleries and virtually no contemporary art market exist in other cities. To boost access to the visual arts in still-isolated Russian provinces, the government's Ministry of Culture is sponsoring annual contemporary arts festivals in provincial cities. Special funds are being set aside to allow host museums to purchase works from the festivals for their own collections.

FOLK ARTS

Visitors to Russia usually seek out traditional Russian arts and crafts, both to view museum quality or antique objects and also to purchase contemporary work. The Russian arts of wood carving, ceramics, lacquerware, weaving, and embroidery, to name but a few, developed as peasants worked at home, both for pleasure and to augment their meager incomes from farming. Their imaginative use of materials and rich decoration give these objects a particular charm. Caucasian folk art includes the well-known knotted carpets and rugs, knitted work, beadwork, pottery, and embroidery.

Common culture also involves rich traditions of story and song. Folk epics, known as *byliny,* were half sung, half spoken, usually by two groups, one group offering an improvised counterpoint to the other. Songs and dances were carried from one village to the next by professional, clown-like entertainers, who were also hired from time to time by the Russian court. Under communism, the traditional folk music and dance became bland and watered down, the effects of having to pass under official scrutiny. Today, Russian folk groups "sing and stomp and yip old village songs with unnerving gusto," [43] as a recent review in the *New York Times* noted. Not only do these groups revive long-forgotten melodies and intricate folk dances, but they also keep alive the history of rural Russia.

CLASSICAL MUSIC AND BALLET

The classics of Russian opera, music, and ballet dominate the stage at St. Petersburg's "White Nights" festival, which takes place every summer during the last weeks of June. The enduring popularity of this great repertoire has helped cultural institutions, like the Bolshoi Ballet, move forward without losing their roots.

Russian composer Mikhail Glinka wrote dramatic, instrumental, and vocal music.

Many of these classics date from the nineteenth and early twentieth centuries, periods of outstanding achievement in the arts. Musicians revere the pioneer in Russian classical music, Mikhail Glinka (1804–1857), who studied opera and music in Italy and Germany and then came back to Russia to compose in the spirit of his homeland. *A Life for the Tsar,* an opera based on the story of a brave Russian peasant who saved the life of the first Romanov tsar, premiered in 1836, earning Glinka a handsome court salary and many new opportunities. The opera was basically a Russian version of the Italian form, incorporating Russian folk melodies. Although Glinka led an undisciplined life, he completed another opera, five orchestral works, chorales, chamber and piano music, and many songs. His work became the foundation for other great composers, who thereafter looked to Russia's great history and folk traditions for inspiration.

Glinka's successor was Mili Balakirev (1836–1910) and his four associates, Cesar Cui (1835–1918), Modest Mussorgsky (1839–1881), Nikolay Rimsky-Korsakov (1844–1908), and Aleksandr Borodin (1833–1887). They formed a music study group in St. Petersburg, along with the critic Vladimir Stasov, that became known as the "Mighty Handful." Despite their musical differences, they all identified with the Russian people and sought to create a national music of distinction.

The brilliant pianist Anton Rubinstein (1829–1894) established the first Russian conservatory in St. Petersburg in 1862; his brother, Nicholas Rubinstein (1835–1881) founded a conservatory in Moscow in 1866. The first graduate of the St. Petersburg Conservatory was none other than Pyotr Tchaikovsky (1841–1893), whose vast output of vocal, orchestral, chamber, ballet, and operatic music is known the world over. The Moscow Conservatory trained Sergey Rachmaninoff (1873–1943), who among other accomplishments created a new literature of Russian piano music. Igor Stravinsky (1882–1971) had a profound impact on twentieth-century music, developing new sounds and techniques based on polyrhythms, polyharmony, polytonality, and a radical orchestral style. Sergey Prokofiev (1891–1953) became a neo-Romantic, with a fondness for classical forms, whose music looks to Brahms, while Dmitri Shostakovich (1906–1975) who lived in conflict with Stalin's regime, wrote within what was now the classic Russian tradition, with strong links to the works of Borodin, Mussorgsky, Tchaikovsky, and Glinka.

THE PERFORMING ARTS

The evolution of the Russian ballet is closely connected to that of music. Ballet dancers were first trained in Russia under the Empresses Anna (ruled 1730–1740) and Elizabeth (ruled 1741–1762) as part of the royal household. A French dancer and choreographer, Charles Didelot, founded a company of 114 ballet dancers in St. Petersburg in 1811, which immediately flourished and laid the foundation of a grand tradition. Didelot's philosophy was that dancing should be "poetry in action," an ideal that remains in place today.

Among the five theaters maintained by the imperial court (two in Moscow, three in St. Petersburg), the Mariinsky Imperial Ballet Theater in St. Petersburg was especially favored. Tchaikovsky's *Sleeping Beauty, Swan Lake,* and *The Nutcracker* are some of the most famous Russian ballets staged there in the 1890s, a decade of magnificent choreography by Marius Petipa (1818–1910) and his assistant, Lev Ivanov (1834–1901).

After Petipa's retirement in 1903, new trends emerged in St. Petersburg under the tutelage of Mikhail Fokine (1880–1942), a young dancer and choreographer and the Mariinsky's new ballet master. The Ballets Russes was formed as an independent company by Sergey Diaghilev (1872–1929), who brought Moscow's and St. Petersburg's dancers to Paris and London and promoted the careers of the great Russian dancers Anna Pavlova (1881–1931), Tamara Karsavina (1885–1978), and Vaslav Nijinsky (1889–1950).

The remarkable artistic ferment of the late nineteenth and early twentieth centuries in Russia also produced K. S. Stanislavsky, who founded the Moscow Art Theater in 1898. Stanislavsky's method of teaching acting adhered to three main principles: respect for the author's intentions, rigorous training to analyze and express character faithfully, and subordination of individual performance to the ensemble. Stage decoration was simple and realistic. The Moscow Art Theater made frequent foreign tours, introducing the "theater of inner feeling" to the rest of the world.

The upheaval and chaos of World War I and the Russian Revolution brought an end to this period of vitality and genius. Although the Russians had lived with various forms of censorship for many generations, the Soviet period was particularly severe and stifling. Cut off from religion and the truth of their own history, workers in the arts were confined to forms of propaganda. Those who refused to conform were ostracized and suffered materially and spiritually. Those who were in favor with the regime one year could find themselves outcasts the next.

Russian Cinema

However, the new art of filmmaking was championed by the Communist Party. Thus the "golden era" of cinema, when the most famous silent films were made, including the director

Anna Pavlova plays the title role in The Dying Swan. *Pavlova performed with both the Mariinsky Imperial Ballet Theater and the Ballets Russes.*

S. M. Eisenstein's (1898–1948) *Potemkin* (1925), quickly evaporated, since movies had to reflect the official Communist doctrine. Eisenstein's style was based on the notion that cinema's power lies in the way it reorders the world through film editing, or montage, not in its ability to document the real world. Stalin, on the other hand, impressed by the power of screen images to influence the public, insisted that "socialist realism" was the only acceptable mode for the state-run film

SERGEY DIAGHILEV (1872–1929)

A versatile, influential promoter of the arts, Sergey Diaghilev not only organized groundbreaking painting exhibitions but also produced concerts, operas, and ballets, bringing together the best artistic talent of his time—dancers, artists, musicians, choreographers, set and costume designers—in unprecedented collaborations.

The son of an army officer who inherited a family estate, Diaghilev grew up in a cultured home surrounded by books, art, and music. Although headed towards a law degree, as a young adult he devoted more attention to music. In 1899 he helped found an influential art journal and obtained a position at the Imperial Theatres for "special projects."

From 1906 on Diaghilev organized events and exhibitions that embraced his wide interests in painting, music, dance, and design. His brilliant and influential ballet company, Ballets Russes, performed in Paris in 1909 and in London in 1911. He staged a series of original and controversial ballets with the composer Igor Stravinsky, including *Firebird* in 1910, *Pétrouchka* in 1911, and *Rite of Spring* in 1913. Other composers with whom he worked included Debussy, Ravel, and Prokofiev. He also commissioned renowned painters such as Benois, Bakst, Matisse, Picasso, and Braque to design sets and costumes.

A disciple of Diaghilev's, George Balanchine (1904–1983), immigrated to the United States and became one of ballet's most revered choreographers.

Sergey Diaghilev in Rite of Spring, *a 1913 ballet.*

industry. Even with these constraints, Eisenstein's *Aleksandr Nevsky* (1938), scored by Prokofiev, is still hailed as one of the great battle movies of all time.

After the death of Stalin a new, fruitful period of filmmaking began. By the 1970s Soviet cinema boasted the highest per capita audience figures in the world. Director Andrey Tarkovsky (1932–1986) earned a worldwide reputation for a total of seven films, including *Andrei Rublev* (1969), which took the great icon painter's life and artistic struggle as its subject. By the 1980s a new group of Russian film directors, including the popular Nikita Mikhalkov, had come to the forefront, exporting vivid and passionate movies that finally are free to take Russia itself as their subject, examining critical points in its history.

DEVELOPMENTS IN LITERATURE

Among the most popular books in Russia in 1997 were self-help books, excerpts from the works of Sigmund Freud, and mystery novels. But the classics of Russian literature still line the shelves of every Russian bookstore. It is through the translation of Russian literature that many people in the West and elsewhere are first exposed to Russian culture.

Throughout the medieval and early modern period, a folk literature of tales and epic songs developed, providing a rich and vital tradition for later writers to draw upon. But not until the nineteenth and early twentieth centuries did Russian literature rise to the highest level of literary achievement.

The great age of Russian letters was ushered in by the poet Aleksandr Pushkin (1799–1837), who had a profound influence on literature and the arts, especially in his themes and characterizations. "By his literary mastery he seemed to prove at one stroke the strength of the native Russian genius,"[44] notes one music historian, who goes on to explain how for the next hundred years Russian composers based compositions on Pushkin's stories, poems, and plays.

Born to an aristocratic family in Moscow, Pushkin died at the age of thirty-seven. In his brief life he wrote more than seven hundred poems and other literary works. His narrative poem *The Bronze Horseman* (1833) is often considered a summary of Pushkin's complex view of Russia's people and their destiny. Other landmark works include *Eugene Onegin* (1823–1830), a verse novel, and *Boris Godunov* (1825), a

Writer Aleksandr Pushkin profoundly influenced Russian literature. Although he died at thirty-seven, Pushkin wrote more than seven hundred poems and other literary works.

tragic drama based on the historical figure, and later the basis for an opera by Mussorgsky. The smoothness, balance, and simplicity of Pushkin's diction displays his mastery of the Russian language. "I don't like grafting European graces and French subtleties onto our old language," Pushkin wrote in a letter in 1823. "Roughness and simplicity suit it better." [45]

THE GREAT RUSSIAN PROSE

The tragedy of Pushkin's death in a duel sparked the career of another young writer, Mikhail Lermontov (1814–1841). Upon hearing the news of Pushkin's fate, Lermontov wrote a poem, *Death of a Poet* (1837), casting blame on the corrupt forces in and around the Russian court that played a role in Pushkin's demise. The poem earned Lermontov a year's exile to the

Caucasus, the details of which would figure largely in his novel *A Hero of Our Time* (1840). The novel consists of five stories, centered on the romantic hero Pechorin, which are presented out of chronological sequence as Pechorin is viewed from various angles. The sophisticated structure and focus on the psychology of the central character anticipates the work of the outstanding novelists to follow.

The first great prose writer after Lermontov was Nikolay Gogol (1809–1852), a friend of Pushkin's from Ukraine who worked in St. Petersburg as a government clerk and teacher. Gogol chose everyday life as the subject of his work, which he imbued with a rare imaginative and stylistic richness. His

Fyodor Dostoyevsky's dark probings of the human psyche and the nature of evil have made his works literary classics.

novel *Dead Souls* (1842) is acclaimed as one of the greatest novels in Russian, and his collections of short stories, including the frequently anthologized "The Overcoat," continue to be held up as a model of the genre.

DOSTOYEVSKY, TOLSTOY, AND CHEKHOV

In the 1820s two of Russia's finest writers were born, Fyodor Dostoyevsky (1821–1881) and Leo Tolstoy (1828–1910). Although these two giants never met each other, together they brought the Russian novel to new heights. The complexity of their biographies rivals that of the characters they created. An aristocrat and heir to a four-thousand-acre estate, Tolstoy never had to worry about his finances. He became the most famous author in his day in Russia, earning abundant royalties from his monumental epic, *War and Peace* (1869), and tragic love story, *Anna Karenina* (1876). In contrast, Dostoyevsky came from a middle-class background and for most of his adult life was never out of debt. Tolstoy spent his twenties at university, in military service, and then traveling to Europe; Dostoyevsky embroiled himself in a socialist group and was sent to a penal colony in Siberia. Interestingly, both men turned to religion to inform the moral core of their work. Tolstoy became known especially as an early champion of nonviolent protest and corresponded with India's political and spiritual leader, Mohandas Gandhi. Dostoyevsky became engrossed in the problems of the loss of faith, sin, suffering, and the possibility of ultimate redemption, the portrayal of which fueled his great novels, including *Crime and Punishment* (1866) and *The Brothers Karamazov* (1880). In 1880, after rereading Dostoyevsky's novel *House of the Dead* (1862), Tolstoy wrote in a letter to a friend, "I do not know of a better book in all modern literature . . . including Pushkin. If you should see Dostoyevsky, tell him that I love him."[46] In 1881, before a meeting could be scheduled, Dostoyevsky suddenly died. Tolstoy survived to the age of eighty-two, dying in 1910 at a small railway station after years of estrangement from his wife.

After Tolstoy, the next brilliant writer to emerge was Anton Chekhov (1860–1904), a physician who wrote stories and sketches to help support himself and his family while he practiced medicine. Chekhov visited Tolstoy in 1895, and the two men became friends; Tolstoy developed an appreciation and affection for Chekhov's stories, saying, "Chekhov is Pushkin in prose."[47] Chekhov deeply admired Tolstoy and learned a great deal from him, but Chekhov also knew he had to forge his own path, which he once described as seeking "something slightly sour," a mood he portrayed with exquisite objectivity. Chekhov's fame in the West rests on performances of his four plays, *The Seagull, Uncle Vanya, Three Sisters,* and *The Cherry Orchard.*

TWENTIETH-CENTURY VOICES

As in the visual arts, under communism official and unofficial literature and literary circles developed. A vast number of Russian writers emigrated, which was a sad but understandable loss to those remaining on Russian soil. Years of exile, imprisonment, and repression shaped the lives of writers bold enough to continue writing critically about the Soviet experience. Control over writers and their literary output began to ease slightly in the late 1950s and 1960s, during the Khrushchev period. A significant breakthrough was made by Aleksandr Solzhenitsyn, who depicted the conditions in Stalin's camps in his landmark novel *One Day in the Life of Ivan Denisovich.* Although Soviet authorities allowed him to accept the Nobel Prize in 1970, three years later he was exiled (an exile he maintained voluntarily until his recent return to Russia). Other Russian winners of the Nobel Prize in literature include Ivan Bunin (1933), Boris Pasternak (1958, prize declined), Mikhail Sholokhov (1965), and Joseph Brodsky (1986).

Formal constraints on literature and contemporary writers did not disappear until glasnost, under Gorbachev. Previously banned books became available, literary journals built circulations in the millions, and new literary prizes were established. The literary horizon in Russia today is open and vast. As in all areas of the arts, new voices are emerging, ready to connect diverse and appreciative audiences.

RUSSIA IN THE
WORLD COMMUNITY

The peaceful collapse of the Soviet Union in 1991 was an important step in a transition of great magnitude. Not only the citizens of the USSR but the world community was forced to adjust to drastic change in the government's basic orientation.

Of foremost concern was the fate of the nuclear arsenal. What would be Russia's nuclear policy? What would happen to the existing nuclear weapons in Russia, Ukraine, Belarus, and Kazakhstan? In 1991 the Soviet Union had roughly thirty thousand nuclear warheads of various types. Since then, American analysts estimate that Russia has been ridding itself of about two thousand warheads a year. Belarus, Kazakhstan, and Ukraine have given up their nuclear capability.

DANGEROUS NUCLEAR MATERIAL

But paradoxically, as Russia's surplus nuclear warheads are dismantled, another problem grows: safeguarding the highly enriched uranium and plutonium from their cores. "There is a common perception that, with the end of the Cold War, the dangers of nuclear weapon materials have decreased. But in many ways the problems of control . . . have grown more serious," concludes a study released in 1997 by the Institute for Science and International Security in Washington, D.C. "Less than one percent of the material produced for military purposes is currently under any form of international verification."[48] There are approximately one hundred weapon storage sites in Russia today.

Russia's program to remove nuclear materials from former Soviet republics, now sovereign nations, has from time to time run into diplomatic snarls. Efforts in 1996 and 1997 to remove a cache of nuclear material from the CIS (Commonwealth of Independent States) republic of Georgia underline some of the problems that have arisen. Stored in an obsolete nuclear reactor outside of Tbilisi, the Georgian capital, the

A WHISTLE-BLOWER'S REPORT ILL RECEIVED

It is no secret that the aging Russian nuclear submarine fleet in the White Sea poses a serious risk of a reactor accident. But when Aleksandr Nikitin, a nuclear engineer and retired captain in the Russian navy, in conjunction with the Norwegian environmental group Bellona, produced a bleak report on the Russian submarine fleet, he was arrested and accused of high treason and espionage. Bellona and Nikitin insisted that their investigations were based on open sources, including newspapers, professional literature, and research reports.

After ten months in custody, Nikitin was released in 1997. However, the charges against him still stand, and Bellona's report remains banned in Russia, the first publication to be prohibited there since the fall of the Soviet Union. Nikitin has been championed by the international human rights organization Amnesty International as a prisoner of conscience.

material was virtually unguarded in the early 1990s during the civil war taking place in this highly volatile region. Arrangements between the United States, Russia, and Georgia to pay for and dispose of the spent fuel hit environmental and legal roadblocks in each of the countries. "American officials said they hoped this issue would ultimately be finessed by having the Georgians sign over legal ownership of the material to Russia,"[49] according to a recent article in the *New York Times*.

THE NEW NUCLEAR ARRANGEMENT

However, important milestones of nuclear cooperation have also transpired. In 1991 Presidents George Bush and Mikhail Gorbachev unilaterally deactivated and withdrew the bulk of their tactical nuclear weapons, acting quickly and without the delays of an official written agreement. The START-1 treaty, signed by President George Bush and Boris Yeltsin in 1992, provided for substantial reduction of warheads on each side. Belarus, Kazakhstan, and Ukraine were also party to the treaty, which requires periodic exchanges of data. In 1996 the five declared nuclear powers (the United States, France, Great Britain, Russia, and China) signed the Comprehensive Test Ban Treaty, guaranteeing that no further nuclear tests will be conducted.

There is an ongoing financial and technical collaboration between Russia and the United States to attend to many important details of disarmament. The United States agreed in 1994 to buy five hundred tons (out of a total of twelve hundred tons) of Russia's highly enriched uranium from dismantled warheads. Over $1 billion in U.S. funds have been authorized for the process of safely taking apart Russian nuclear weapons, although the Clinton administration has announced a cutoff date of 2001 for this program.

The START-2 treaty, calling for further cuts on each side's strategic weapons and ratified in the U.S. Senate in 1996, stalled in Russia's Duma but is expected to be ratified by the end of 1997. Unofficial estimates calculate the cost to Russia of implementing the treaty at as much as $7.5 billion. Continued technical and financial support from the United States will be critical to enable Russia to comply with the treaty. A new series of talks to design START-3 is expected, perhaps even before Russia ratifies START-2.

In 1991 Soviet president Mikhail Gorbachev (pictured) and U.S. president George Bush dismantled many of their nations' tactical nuclear weapons.

Russia has also agreed to close down its remaining plutonium-producing reactors by the year 2000, providing it can replace them with alternative energy sources. And there is a continuing effort to improve security at various nuclear installations and work out terms for the safe management of nuclear waste. Nuclear scientists from Russia, the United States, France, Germany, and other countries meet in forums such as NATO's (North Atlantic Treaty Organization) Advanced Research Workshop to address issues relating to the dismantled nuclear warheads and the protection, control, and accountability of nuclear materials.

A group of Russian soldiers trains in front of a vehicle designed to launch long-range nuclear missiles. Presidents Clinton and Yeltsin continue to negotiate treaties regarding nuclear weaponry.

RUSSIA AND NATO

In 1993, Poland, Hungary, and the Czech Republic raised the issue of joining NATO. Russia's attitude towards this issue has been inconsistent, influenced by the pressure of nationalist politicians in the Duma who are virulently opposed to Russia's former allies becoming closer partners with the West. The issue was put off for a few years by NATO's "Partnership for Peace" program of 1994, whose goals are enhancing po-

litical and military cooperation throughout Europe and providing a channel for former Soviet bloc nations to be directly involved with NATO. Twenty-six countries, including the Russian Federation, the Baltic republics, much of Eastern and Central Europe, and a number of CIS republics, are members of this forum.

In 1996, U.S. president Bill Clinton endorsed the idea of early membership for Poland, Hungary, and the Czech Republic. To ease Russia's concerns NATO negotiated a special charter with Russia providing security guarantees, including a NATO promise not to deploy nuclear weapons in new member states. NATO has also said that it has no intention of stationing new ground-combat forces in former Warsaw Pact nations. Although there are many details under scrutiny, the new partnership with NATO will give Russia high-level representation and a voice in, although not a veto over, NATO affairs.

Aside from its relationship to NATO, Russia has also taken steps to forge new relationships with other world organizations. In 1997 Russia made a formal proposal to join the World Trade Organization (WTO), the international body that sets up rules of trade between nations. One of the principles of the WTO is to encourage fair competition in trade by reducing protectionism (tariffs or surcharges on imported goods). To join the WTO, Russia will have to lower its average tariff on goods by 10 percent in 1998 to comply with WTO standards.

Russia also participates in G-7 summits, where the seven leading industrial democracies discuss issues of development, international finance, and trade. The group, informally called "G-7 plus one" is expected to eventually become G-8. Furthermore, Russia is taking steps to join the world's leading consortium of banks and another consortium of creditor nations. By striving to meet the requirements of a full partnership in these international organizations, Russia will continue to transform its economy and society, attracting foreign investment, developing markets for Russian goods, and moving closer to the attitudes and policies of other democratic, developed nations.

THE NEAR ABROAD

Of foremost importance to Russia's foreign policy today is its relationship to the "near abroad," the ex-Soviet states that ring Russia, including the Baltic states of Latvia, Estonia, and Lithuania, and the eleven other countries belonging to the CIS: Ukraine, Belarus, Georgia, Armenia, Azerbaijan, Moldova, Kazakhstan, Turkmenistan, Uzbekistan, Kyrgyzstan, and Tajikistan. A series of interlocking border, trade, and economic development arrangements connect Russia to these countries, but the Kremlin of the Russian Federation is not the Kremlin of the old Soviet Union. Russia is still in the process of defining its policies, and numerous complexities have arisen with regard to Russia's evolving status with these newly independent neighbors.

Since the inception of the Commonwealth of Independent States, Russia has led the group and at times advocated a military alliance that would oppose NATO. However, the CIS has never granted itself powers to enforce one member's decisions on another, and it is not likely to do so. Russia's leadership is under scrutiny, as CIS members are demanding that the organization be "a community of equals, in which each country has an identical voice regardless of its size and population," [50] as Ukrainian president Leonid Kuchma said on the eve of a CIS summit meeting in 1997.

THE BALTIC NATIONS

Before World War II, the three Baltic nations of Estonia, Latvia, and Lithuania had made significant headway in becoming modern industrial economies with democratic institutions. Always unwilling Soviet partners—separated from the Russians by religion (a large percentage are Lutheran or Roman Catholic), language, and culture—today the three states share a widespread popular desire to reintegrate into Western Europe and have done so rapidly. Each of these countries has adhered to disciplined fiscal and financial policies in pursuit of economic reform, including privatization and free trade.

However, Russian interests still count in the Baltics. Although no longer as dependent on Russia for trade as they once were, trade with Russia is still important to their economies. The Baltic states also have significant Russian populations within their own borders. Since these countries were the first of the former Soviet republics to go their own way, Russia remains sensitive to and wary of the Baltics' Western focus. The Baltics are likely to spurn any sign of

Russian bullying, but at the same time, should a real crisis arise, they have only an ill-equipped and poorly maintained military to back them. NATO membership may be in the not-too-distant future for Estonia, Lithuania, and Latvia, a bitter pill for Russia to swallow.

UKRAINE AND MOLDOVA

Ukraine is a cornerstone of the CIS, the second-largest state in the commonwealth and potentially one of the richest and most productive. But given the turbulent historic relationship between Russia and Ukraine, which includes Stalin's ruthless terror campaigns that decimated Ukraine's intellectual classes and caused brutal famines, it is not surprising that even today relations are not smooth. Russia and Ukraine face a series of prickly issues, including the status of Sevastopol, the naval base and Black Sea port which has a large Russian population; the fate of the former Soviet Union's Black Sea fleet of warships; and the future of Russian

A fallen monument to Lenin is left to become part of the landscape in Riga, Latvia. Latvia, like the other Baltic nations, was quick to realign with Europe and abandon its ties to Russia.

influence in the Crimea. Six years after independence, Ukraine still cannot get Russia to agree on the border between the two countries. Ukraine has chosen to stay out of new agreements between the Russian Federation and other CIS countries, shunning closer political and military ties. "Ukraine principally opposes attempts to restore the former Soviet Union in any form,"[51] stated a 1996 press release from the Ukrainian Ministry of Foreign Affairs.

However, the economies of Ukraine and Russia are still intertwined, as they have been for centuries. At present, Ukraine's economy is in poor condition, crippled by its 90 percent dependence on Russian fuel supplies, which have been cut drastically since 1992, and Russian trade, which has dwindled but still accounts for almost half of all Ukraine's trade. Graft, corruption, tax evasion, bribery, and bureaucratic red tape are Ukraine's lingering legacies from the old Soviet regime. In 1995 Ukraine began to implement a privatization program to transfer eight thousand medium- and large-scale enterprises to the private sector. The government is encouraging foreign trade and investment, though it has not attracted nearly as much foreign capital as it would like. Ukraine has also reached out to the West for economic aid and is now the third-largest recipient of aid from the United States (trailing only Israel and Egypt).

The United States and Ukraine have signed a series of bilateral agreements designed to support and enhance eco-

RUSSIAN MILITARY IN DECLINE

Lacking adequate resources for food, housing, training, and salaries, the teetering Russian military made headlines in 1996 and 1997. If back wages were not paid, Russian generals feared the army would stop performing its duties.

Political wrangling has delayed urgent reforms that would cut bureaucratic waste, target spending on priority areas, and over the long term transform the conscript-based forces into a leaner, more professional army. Military reform and reductions are national security issues in Russia, because an unstable, underfunded army could be a threat to the integrity of the Russian Federation. Russia's sparsely populated, resource-rich eastern territories are of particular concern because of their proximity to China.

nomic, technical, environmental, and cultural cooperation. Ukraine has been an active participant in NATO's "Partnership for Peace" program, and it has supported the expansion of NATO membership, much to Moscow's chagrin. "Moscow understands that if Ukraine undertakes successful economic reforms, it will loosen its ties with Russia in favor of closer integration with the West,"[52] summarizes Sergei Grigoriev in the *Harvard International Review*. However, Ukraine seems determined to establish a buffer status, trying to work its relationship with both Russia and the West to its own advantage, as best it can.

Ukraine's neighbor to the west, Moldova, looks more towards its ethnic-kin western neighbor, Romania, than to Russia. A law has been passed which will make Romanian the official language in Moldova. Moldova imports all of its oil, coal, and natural gas supplies, and energy shortages have contributed to a sharp economic decline, although the country has made progress on its reform agenda. A separatist movement in the Trans-Dniester region, where the population is 40 percent Moldovan, 28 percent Ukrainian, and 23 percent Russian, strained relations with Russia, but a cease-fire has been in place since 1992. Moldova has offered the region broad cultural and political autonomy.

BELARUS

In contrast to Ukraine's rocky, independent course, Belarus, which was once ruled by the princes of Kiev and also has age-old ties to Russia, is pushing for a place directly under Russia's umbrella. The armed forces of Belarus are already subordinate to Russian military leaders. Belarus has avoided building a capitalist economy in favor of Soviet-style central command economic and political control. But the economy has stagnated, inflation is high, and the currency may collapse. Belarus president Aleksandr Lukashenko has made reunification with Russia his priority and has banned pro-independence demonstrations. Thousands of people continue to participate in illegal demonstrations against the government, leading to roundups and detentions of opposition leaders, followed by closed-door trials. In 1997 the United States suspended all aid to Belarus because of the country's failure to meet human rights standards. A further breakdown of diplomatic relations occurred

Russian president Boris Yeltsin (right) and Belarus president Aleksandr Lukashenko grasp hands. Lukashenko has made it clear that he wants to reunify with Russia.

with back-and-forth expulsions of diplomats from both nations, and the U.S. ambassador has been recalled.

Russia and Belarus have announced plans to align their economies and have already taken steps to unify their customs and border controls. A further step under consideration is for Belarus to give up its own currency in favor of the Russian ruble, a move which would prove expensive to Russia. The dictatorial politics and nostalgia for Soviet times that hold sway in Belarus could be disruptive in Russia, where today's liberal leaders wish to hold on to their reform-minded constituencies. Whether the Russian government will actually take on and bail out Belarus, and whether Belarus will make required economic and legislative reforms, remains to be seen.

THE TRANSCAUCASUS

A fulcrum all its own between Europe and Asia, Russia and the Middle East, the three newly independent countries of the Transcaucasus—Armenia, Azerbaijan, and Georgia—have been dogged by ethnic upheaval, poverty, and political instability. The flash point between Armenia and Azerbaijan is Nagorno-Karabakh, the ethnic Armenian enclave within Azerbaijan that voted to secede and join Armenia in 1988. Russia mediated a cease-fire, which has been in effect since 1994, but more than a million people remain displaced and fifteen thousand lost their lives in the conflict.

In another ethnic conflict, in Georgia, Russian peace-keeping forces still ensure the physical separation between combatants in the regions of South Ossetia and Abkhazia. Georgian president Edward Shevardnadze, the former Soviet foreign minister, has been an efficient and democratic leader, shepherding Georgia to functioning statehood. How-ever, dependence on Russian security has also meant a weakening of Georgian sovereignty.

Azerbaijan is the largest, most populous of the three Trans-caucasus republics, and it has attracted worldwide interest because of the oil reserves in and around the Caspian Sea. Its relationship to Russia has been troubled. For years Azerbai-jan has angrily pointed to Soviet and then Russian military equipment, supplies, and training sent to Armenia, despite Russia's role in mediating the conflict. In response, Azerbaijan has drawn closer to Turkey and Iran. The Azeris speak a Turkic language and most are Muslim. Also, a large population of ethnic Azeris live in northern Iran.

Georgian president Edward Shevardnadze has led Georgia to independence, though his nation is still dependent on Russia for military protection.

The location and control of Azerbaijan's soon-to-be-built pipelines has been the subject of ongoing negotiation since 1994, when a consortium of foreign companies signed an $8 billion deal to develop three offshore fields near Baku. Existing oil pro-duction has been in decline; the local population has yet to benefit from the esti-mated 68 billion barrels under the sea.

The Caspian Sea itself has been the cen-ter of the debate. Azerbaijan and Kazakh-stan say it is a sea. Russia has long argued that it is a lake, which in legal terms would entitle all the surrounding states to shared ownership. Russia pressured Azerbaijan by restricting trade to the capital city, Baku, along the Dagestan–Caspian Sea road and rail routes on the pretext of heightened Russian security needs arising from the war in Chechnya.

In 1997 Azerbaijan announced that Caspian oil would flow through a dual pipeline plan, using the existing Russian pipeline to Novorossiysk, and then building a Georgian pipeline route to Supsa, on Georgia's Black Sea coast, rather than through Armenia and Turkey. This decision favors Russia, which has plenty of influence in Georgia. It also indicates that Azerbaijan, while exploring the benefits of ties to Iran and Turkey, is too weak to resist Russian economic leverage. "[Azerbaijan] cannot afford to depend on Iran, which has its own hegemonic aspirations regarding Azeris; and Turkey, though politically supportive, is not powerful enough to be

Azeris work on an aging oil-drilling rig. Azerbaijan has been instrumental in building a pipeline route through Georgia to the Black Sea coast.

decisive,"[53] explains David E. Mark in the journal *Foreign Policy*. Azerbaijan oil is expected to begin pumping through Russia by the end of 1997.

THE CENTRAL ASIAN STATES

On the northeastern side of the Caspian Sea, Kazakhstan awaits pipeline transportation for its enormous untapped oil reserves in the Tengiz fields. Russia controls a large percentage of equity in the Caspian Pipeline Consortium, which also includes Kazakhstan, Oman, and eight private oil firms. The 990-mile pipeline from Tengiz to Russia's Black Sea oil export outlet at Novorossiysk will have an enormous capacity, initially 28 million metric tons a year, with an expected peak of 67 million metric tons a year.

Turkmenistan is also rich in fossil fuels, but it currently is a poor country largely dependent on Russia and its plans to transport the fuel to market. Uzbekistan is not as richly endowed as Kazakhstan and Turkmenistan, but it has enormous gold deposits (one-quarter of the old Soviet Union's reserves) and is one of the world's leading cotton growers. Kyrgyzstan, a poor, mountainous country with a predominantly agricultural economy, has been one of the most progressive of the former Soviet republics in carrying out market reforms.

In summary, all of the Central Asian republics have historic and current bonds with Russia and will continue to work within the CIS. But they may also explore options beyond Russia for help in exploiting their resources. Exactly when, how, and what price the world benefits from Caspian oil, and to what degree Russia will influence the outcome of those arrangements, is yet to be determined.

SINO-RUSSIAN RELATIONS

Once the long border between the Soviet Union and China was one of the most tense in the world; today Russia and China boast "a strategic partnership," signed in 1996 and setting ambitious targets for Russian-Chinese trade, economic enterprises, and military cooperation. Courting China may balance NATO expansion, from the Russian point of view. But despite the smiling faces, handshakes, and back patting, there remain serious questions about whether or not China and Russia can share the same goals.

The border itself symbolizes the potential for conflict. Only 8 million of Russia's citizens live in the Russian Far East. The Far East and Siberia are the richest regions in valuable resources (coal, oil, timber, metals, diamonds, fisheries, and hydropower) and the least developed in infrastructure. In the Chinese region directly across the border from the Russian Far East live 120 million Chinese (of China's total population of 1.2 billion). Any joint large-scale development project will require labor neither Asiatic nor European Russia can muster but China is willing and able to provide. Up to a half million Chinese laborers are currently immigrating to the Russian Far East from northern China. This looming demographic pressure makes working out a cooperative relationship with China ever more important to Russia. "The pressures of the market and the open frontier will over time subject the region to a thoroughgoing Sinicization, transforming the region and its links with both Moscow and Beijing," [54] according to Sherman Garnett, senior associate at the Carnegie Endowment for International Peace.

Neither side has anything to gain from a military conflict or could take comfort in instability in such vast neighboring areas. Over the long term, Russia will need other strong allies to bolster its position in relation to China. "If Russian foreign policy regains coherence, Russia's new links to China will eventually proceed hand in hand with an outreach to Japan, the United States, and other Pacific and Asian nations," [55] writes Garnett.

INTERNATIONAL CONCERNS

The Soviet Union came apart after a long and painful history that affected generations of Russian citizens. The move to embrace democracy and reform came from inside Russia itself. The rejection of communism and the permanent state of mobilization that communist ideology sanctioned went hand in hand with ordinary people seeking improvements in the everyday quality of their lives. But economic and political reform has produced its own set of hardships and frustrations. Full integration in the world economy will help the new Russian government satisfy the basic needs of their liberal constituencies. The Russian Federation looks to the United States for help in promoting these efforts. The United States has a national security interest in the very same thing. Though tensions between the two powers may arise from time to time, a broader view assures the benefits of a cooperative relationship.

Some friction has resulted from certain Russian foreign policy interests that have clashed with U.S. interests and may again in the future. For instance, Russia has been trying to get the United Nations embargo on Iraqi oil sales lifted because the oil revenue is the only way Iraq can pay Russia for arms purchased from the Soviet Union, a $10 billion debt that Russia needs to collect. In 1997 Russia and Iraq signed a contract to develop oil fields in southern Iraq, believed to hold up to 8 billion barrels of oil. "The agreement will be implemented independently of the lifting of economic sanctions," [56] according to the Russian Energy Ministry.

COLD WAR SPACE TECHNOLOGY IN THE POST–COLD WAR AGE

The Russian space program has suffered a number of setbacks in recent years. The Mir space station suffered nerve-wracking malfunctions in 1997, and a cargo craft collision robbed the orbital outpost of a science lab and half its power. In 1996, Russia was left without a single working photo-reconnaissance satellite in space for several months, and its $300 million Mars mission ended in a dramatic failure. Russia's financial woes also caused delays in 1997 in the building of a planned international space station in conjunction with the United States.

However, one bright light over the Russian sky is the development of a wide variety of cheap and powerful liquid-fuel rocket engines during the years of the cold war, which are used for commercial launchings today. In a series of new partnerships with major aerospace players around the globe, Russian ideas, engines, and vehicles are being sought to launch a new generation of commercial communications satellites.

A Russian cosmonaut and American astronaut shake hands shortly after U.S. space shuttle Atlantis *and Russia's Mir Space Station linked in space in 1995. Since the breakup of the Soviet Union, Russia's space program has suffered several setbacks.*

The United States and other Western governments are also concerned about an Iranian-Russian agreement to construct two nuclear energy plants in Iran, with by-products that could fuel nuclear bombs. Also, Russian arms sales to Iran have prompted other Middle Eastern states to expand their defensive arsenals. "This is a market that has gone out of control," [57] cautions Kenneth Timmerman, director of the Middle East Data Project.

RUSSIA AND THE UNITED STATES: THE NEXT PHASE

Despite the inevitable disagreements, the long-term forecast for U.S.-Russian relations appears calm. U.S. assistance to Russia funds a variety of programs in these key areas: private-sector development, privatization and enterprise restructuring, trade and investment, democracy initiatives, energy, health care, housing, environment, and the safe and secure dismantling of nuclear weapons. Humanitarian assistance represented the major portion of U.S. aid during the initial transition phase in Russia, when there was a pressing need for food, medicine, and other essentials. U.S. efforts now concentrate on technical assistance and direct support for trade and investment.

It is clear that neither the United States nor Russia has a desire for a "cold peace" to replace the cold war. More Russians are visiting the United States than ever before, and vice versa. The American embassy in Moscow issued almost one hundred thousand visas in 1996, twenty times as many as a decade earlier.

The isolation of the communist era has faded away, to be replaced by a host of unprecedented opportunities for Russia and its people. Just as ordinary people were finally able to bring down an empire, so may ordinary people, using the tools of increased commerce and communication, bridge the gap which seemed like an abyss only a generation ago.

FACTS ABOUT RUSSIA

THE GOVERNMENT

Official name: Russian Federation

Form of government: Federation

Capital city: Moscow

Administrative divisions: The Russian Federation includes 21 autonomous republics, 49 provinces (oblasts), six territories *(krai)*, and 10 national districts *(okrugs)*.

Date of independence: August 24, 1991, from the Soviet Union

Date of constitution: December 12, 1993

Voting age: 18

NATIONAL HOLIDAYS

January 1	New Year's Day
January 7	Russian Orthodox Christmas
March 8	International Women's Day
May 1	Formerly, Workers International Solidarity Day, now celebrated informally as Spring Holiday
May 9	Victory Day
June 12	Independence Day of Russia (the date the Russian Congress declared Russia's sovereignty)
October 7	Constitution Day

PEOPLE

Total population: 147,987,000 (1997 estimate)

Population growth rate: −.05% (1997 estimate)

Population density: 23 persons per square mile (9 per sq. km.)

Population over 65: 12%

Population under 15: 21%

Birth rate: 11 births/1,000 population

Death rate: 16 deaths/1,000 population

Life expectancy:

At birth: 63.8 years
Infant deaths per 1,000 live births: 24
Male: 56.51 years
Female: 70.31 years

Ethnicity: Russian 81.5%, Tatar 3.8%, Ukrainian 3%, Chuvash 1.2%, Bashkir 0.9%, Belorussian 0.8%, Moldavian 0.7%, other 8.1%

Population of the USSR in 1991: 292 million
Literacy rate: Nearly 100%

POPULATION OF THE RUSSIAN EMPIRE 1200–1910

Year	Population
1200	7,500,000
1725	1,550,000
1812	43,000,000
1860	60,000,000
1897	124,200,000
1905	130,000,000
1910	160,800,000

POPULATION OF RUSSIA

Year	Population	Year	Population
1950	101,937,000	1996	148,178,000
1960	119,632,000	1997	147,987,000
1970	130,245,000	1998	147,791,000
1980	139,045,000	1999	147,799,000
1990	148,081,000	2000	147,938,000
1991	148,457,000	2010	149,978,000
1992	148,591,000	2020	149,632,000
1993	148,506,000	2030	149,111,000
1994	148,363,000	2040	147,148,000
1995	148,291,000	2050	142,887,000

POPULATION GROWTH

Period	Growth Rate
1950–1960	1.6%
1960–1970	0.9%
1970–1980	0.7%
1980–1990	0.6%
1990–2000	0.0%
2000–2010	0.1%
2010–2020	0.0%
2020–2030	0.0%
2030–2040	−0.1%
2040–2050	−0.3%

LAND

Land area: 6,592,665 square miles, the largest state in the world

Highest point: Mount Elbrus, a peak in the Caucasus; at 18,510 ft., also the highest mountain in Europe

Lowest point: Caspian Sea (–92 ft.)

Longest river: Ob River (2,287 miles)

Largest freshwater lake: Lake Baikal (12,162 square miles)

Coastline: 26,582 miles

Maritime borders: Atlantic Ocean; Baltic, Barents, Black, and Caspian Seas; Arctic Ocean; Pacific Ocean

Land borders: Norway, Finland, Estonia, Latvia, Lithuania, Poland, Belarus, Ukraine, Georgia, Azerbaijan, Kazakhstan, Mongolia, China, North Korea. Separated from the United States (Alaska) by the 56-mile-wide Bering Strait, from Japan by the 14-mile-wide Nemuro Strait

Exclave: The city of Kaliningrad, separated from the rest of the country by Belarus and Lithuania.

NATURAL REGIONS

Arctic zone: In the extreme north, the ground is frozen year round. Contains several mountainous zones.

Tundra zone: From the borders with Norway and Finland in the west to the Bering Sea in the east. Permanently frozen ground (permafrost) lies underneath topsoil, which thaws in the summer. Vegetation includes dwarf shrubs, berry bushes, mosses, lichens, and carpets of flowers in the summer. Dwarf trees are common in the southern margins, known as the tundra forest.

Forest (taiga) zone: Occupies about two-thirds of Russia, stretches across the entire country, and is the world's largest nontropical forest area. Pine, spruce, fir, and larch are the most common trees.

Steppe (grassland) zone: Widest in European Russia and southeastern Siberia. This is also the region of the rich black soil *(chernozem)*.

Subtropical zone: A small area on the southwestern coast of the Black Sea, where the average winter temperatures remain above freezing.

CLIMATE

Except for the marginal areas, Russia's climate is generally cool to cold. Winters are mildest in the southwest along the Black Sea, and most severe in the heart of northeast Siberia, where the average temperature in January is –58 F (–51 C). Summers are hottest in southeast European Russia, in southwest Siberia, and in some of the valleys of south-central Siberia, where temperatures may rise above 100 F (38 C).

ECONOMY

Monetary unit: ruble; $1 equaled 5,683 rubles in 1997

Rate of inflation: 22% (1996 est.)

GDP: $721.2 billion (1994 World Bank est.)

Per capita government expenditures: $4,792

Imports: $35.7 billion (1994 est.); including machinery and equipment, chemicals, consumer goods, grain, meat

Exports: $48 billion (1994 est.); including petroleum and petroleum products, natural gas, wood and wood products, coal, nonferrous metals, chemicals, civilian and military manufactures

Mineral resources: oil, natural gas, coal, iron ore, gold, platinum, diamonds, silver, mercury, nickel, chromium, bauxite, copper, lead, tin, zinc, tungsten, cobalt, molybdenum, uranium, asbestos, phosphates, potassium, and salt

Chief crops: grain, potatoes, sugar beets, vegetables, sunflowers

Major industries: extraction and processing of raw materials, arms and weaponry, chemicals, synthetic fibers, rubber, plastics, building materials, electronics, timber, paper, textile, clothing, footwear

Trade: An extensive network of trading partners, including the CIS countries, Western and Eastern Europe, the United Kingdom, the United States, Japan, China, India, and others

CHRONOLOGY

B.C.
ca. 800–200
The Scythians occupy the steppe.

200 –A.D. 200
The Sarmatians replace the Scythians on the steppe.

A.D.
98
A Slavic tribe is noted and described by Tacitus.

200–400
Goths invade the western steppe.

400–550
Huns expel the Goths.

558
Avars invade southern Russia and the steppe.

600
Slavic tribes expand to modern-day Germany, the Balkan Peninsula, and Greece.

650
Khazars establish kingdom and control the steppe.

750
Khazars convert to Judaism.

793
Scandinavian Vikings (called Varangians in Rus) begin to migrate.

860
Varangians seize Kiev from the Khazars and attack Constantinople.

862
Rurik becomes ruler of Novgorod, establishing a dynasty.

882
Oleg makes Kiev his capital.

962
Svyatoslav rules, first leader of Rus with a Slavic name.

977
Novgorod breaks away from Kiev.

988
Vladimir I converts to Eastern Christianity.

1019–1054
Yaroslav is grand prince of Kiev.

1037
First Metropolitanate is installed at Kiev.

1147
First mention of Moscow in the *Primary Chronicle.*

1169
Kiev is sacked by Andrei Bogolyubsky, grand prince of Vladimir.

1223
A Russian-Polovetsian force is defeated by the Mongols (Tatars).

1237–1240
Batu Khan completes Mongol conquest of Rus.

1252–1263
Alexander Nevsky is grand prince of Vladimir.

1325–1340
Ivan I of Moscow becomes grand prince under the khans.

1325
Moscow becomes the seat of the Metropolitanate.

1378
Prince Dimitry defeats a Tatar army at Battle of Kulikovo.

1452
Vasily II stops paying Tatar tribute.

1471–1477
Novgorod attacked by Ivan III, grand prince of Moscow.

1472
Ivan III marries Sophia Paleologus, from Byzantium.

1480
Close of the Tatar period of rule.

1552
Kazan conquered by Ivan IV of Muscovy.

1556
Astrakhan conquered by Ivan IV.

1564
Ivan IV leaves Moscow and forms an *oprichnina.*

1583
First Russian settlement in Siberia.

1613
First Romanov crowned tsar.

1637
Russians reach the Pacific.

1649
Freedom of movement for serfs forbidden.

1653
Last full meeting of the assembly, the *zemsky sobor.*

1654–1667
Russo-Polish War over Ukraine.

1697
Peter the Great's "Grand Embassy" makes its trip
to Europe.

1703
The founding of St. Petersburg by Peter the Great.

1709
Russia defeats Sweden at the Battle of Poltava in Ukraine.

1762
Nobility emancipated from service obligation.

1772
Peasant revolt led by Cossack leader Pugachev.

1795
Final partition of Poland; Russia gains Crimea.

1801
Beginning of conquest of the Caucasus.

1805
Entry into coalition against France.

1809
Parts of Finland ceded to Russia by Sweden.

1812
Napoléon's invasion of Russia; burning of Moscow
by its inhabitants.

1814
Tsar Alexander pursues Napoléon to Paris, enters the
city in triumph.

1825
Decembrist Uprising, following the death of Alexander I.

1853–1856
Crimean War fought between Russia and an alliance of
Turkey, Great Britain, and France.

1860
Vladivostok founded.

1861
Emancipation Manifesto frees serfs.

1867
Alaska sold to the United States.

1881
Assassination of Alexander II.

1891
Building begins of Trans-Siberian railroad.

1901
Socialist Revolutionary Party established.

1903
Mensheviks and Bolsheviks split.

1904–1905
Russo-Japanese War.

1905
Bloody Sunday and October Manifesto.

1906
First Duma opens and closes.

1914
World War I begins.

1917
Tsar Nicholas II abdicates; Russian Revolution.

1918
Moscow renamed capital of Soviet Union;
Red Terror begins.

1922
Union of Soviet Socialist Republics (USSR) formed.

1928
First Five-Year Plan is implemented.

1932–1933
Famine devastates Ukraine.

1936
Stalin begins political purges.

1939
Stalin signs nonaggression pact with Nazi Germany;
World War II begins.

1941
Germany invades the Soviet Union.

1941–1944
Siege of Leningrad.

1945
World War II ends.

1956
Khrushchev denounces Stalin in secret speech;
Hungarian uprising crushed.

1957
Sputnik, first artificial satellite, launched; competition
between United States and USSR intensifies.

1962
Cuban missile crisis heightens cold war tensions.

1968
Red Army suppresses "Prague Spring" liberalism in Czechoslovakia.

1971
USSR launches first manned space station.

1972
SALT I agreement between the United States and the USSR to limit nuclear weapons.

1979
SALT II signed; Soviet invasion of Afghanistan.

1985
Glasnost becomes Gorbachev's new policy.

1986
Chernobyl nuclear power plant disaster.

1990
Lithuania declares independence from the USSR.

1991
A coup to take control from Gorbachev is attempted and fails; USSR dissolved.

1992
Signing of Russian Federation treaty by eighteen autonomous republics.

1993
Constitution of the Russian Federation.

NOTES

CHAPTER 1:
THE FIRST RUSSIA: LAND OF THE SLAVIC PEOPLE

1. Quoted in Rhoda Hoff, *Russia: Adventures in Eyewitness History*. New York: Henry Z. Walck, 1964, p. 2.

2. Tacitus, *Germania*. Cambridge, MA: Harvard University Press, 1970, p. 213.

3. Quoted in Warren B. Walsh, ed., *Readings in Russian History from Ancient Times to the Post-Stalin Era*, vol. 1. Syracuse, NY: Syracuse University Press, 1963, p. 19.

4. Quoted in Walsh, *Readings in Russian History*, vol. 1, p. 19.

5. John Lawrence, *A History of Russia*. New York: Penguin Books, 1993, p. 25.

6. Quoted in Walsh, *Readings in Russian History*, vol. 1, p. 23.

7. Quoted in Walsh, *Readings in Russian History*, vol. 1, p. 24.

8. Quoted in Walsh, *Readings in Russian History*, vol. 1, p. 25.

9. Quoted in Walsh, *Readings in Russian History*, vol. 1, p. 26.

10. Quoted in Robert Wallace, *Rise of Russia*. New York: Time-Life Books, 1967, p. 32.

11. Quoted in George Vernadsky, ed., *A Source Book for Russian History from Early Times to 1917*, vol. 1. New Haven, CT: Yale University Press, 1972, p. 33.

12. Quoted in Walsh, *Readings in Russian History*, vol. 1, p. 50.

13. Quoted in Vernadsky, *A Source Book for Russian History*, vol. 1, p. 46.

CHAPTER 2: THE SECOND RUSSIA: AN IMPERIAL VISION

14. Quoted in Jesse D. Clarkson, *A History of Russia*. New York: Random House, 1961, p. 78.

15. Quoted in Vernadsky, *A Source Book for Russian History*, vol. 1, p. 56.

16. Quoted in Basil Dmytryshyn, ed., *Medieval Russia: A Source Book, 900–1700.* New York: Holt, Rinehart and Winston, 1967, p. 211.

17. Quoted in Vernadsky, *A Source Book for Russian History,* vol. 1, p. 178.

18. Quoted in Dmytryshyn, *Medieval Russia,* p. 256.

19. Quoted in Paul Avrich, *Russian Rebels: 1600–1800.* New York: Schocken Books, 1972, p. 132.

20. Quoted in Avrich, *Russian Rebels,* p. 140.

21. Quoted in Vernadsky, *A Source Book for Russian History,* vol. 2, pp. 425–26.

22. Quoted in Vernadsky, *A Source Book for Russian History,* vol. 2, p. 582.

23. Quoted in Vernadsky, *A Source Book for Russian History,* vol. 2, p. 589.

CHAPTER 3: THE THIRD RUSSIA: THE COMMUNIST VISION

24. Quoted in Richard Pipes, *A Concise History of the Russian Revolution.* New York: Knopf, 1995, p. 88.

25. Quoted in Pipes, *A Concise History,* p. 117.

26. Quoted in Pipes, *A Concise History,* p. 118.

27. Quoted in Pipes, *A Concise History,* p. 164.

28. Paul Johnson, *Modern Times: The World from the Twenties to the Eighties.* New York: Harper & Row, 1983, p. 271.

29. Quoted in Peter Neville, *A Traveller's History of Russia and the USSR.* New York: Interlink Books, 1994, p. 212.

30. Quoted in Neville, *A Traveller's History of Russia,* p. 233.

31. Quoted in Robert Andrews, ed., *The Columbia Dictionary of Quotations.* New York: Columbia University Press, 1993, p. 346.

32. Quoted in Andrews, *The Columbia Dictionary,* p. 166.

CHAPTER 4: THE NEW RUSSIA

33. Avraham Shama, "Inside Russia's True Economy," *Foreign Policy,* Summer 1996. Reference #A18358007 from Magazine Database Plus (CompuServe Information Service).

34. Quoted in Shama, "Inside Russia's True Economy." Reference #A18358007 from Magazine Database Plus (CompuServe Information Service).

35. Quoted in Vanora Bennet, "Russia: Crime Pays, the State Doesn't," *Los Angeles Times,* November 28, 1996, home edition. Downloaded from the Publications Library of The Wall Street Journal Interactive edition at www.wsj.com.

36. Quoted in "Godfather of the Kremlin: Russian Crime Boss Boris Berezovsky," *Forbes,* December 30, 1996. Reference #A18965441 from Magazine Database Plus (CompuServe Information Service).

37. Quoted in "That Charging Bear Is a Russian Bull (Market)," *Baron's,* March 10, 1997. Downloaded from the Publications Library of The Wall Street Journal Interactive edition at www.wsj.com.

38. Richard Layard and John Parker, *The Coming Russian Boom.* New York: Free Press, 1996, p. 121.

39. Quoted in "Solzhenitsyn: Russia Joining Third World," *Reuters Limited,* March 23, 1997. Downloaded from www.yahoo.com/headlines/.

40. Quoted in "Still Going for Gold," *Russian Life,* July 1996. Reference #A18680770 from Magazine Database Plus (CompuServe Information Service).

CHAPTER 5:
ARTS AND TRADITIONS: BINDING OLD AND NEW

41. Olga Listosova, "The Holy Image Makers," *Russian Life,* December 1996. Reference #A19225888 from Magazine Database Plus (CompuServe Information Service).

42. Suzanne Massie, *Land of the Firebird: The Beauty of Old Russia.* New York: Simon and Schuster, 1980, p. 137.

43. Alessandra Stanley, "From Russia, with Songs of Days Long Gone, to the U.S.," *New York Times,* April 1, 1997, p. C11.

44. Richard Leonard, *A History of Russian Music.* New York: Macmillan, 1957, p. 38.

45. Quoted in William Rose Benét, ed., *The Reader's Encyclopedia.* New York: Thomas Y. Crowell, 1965, p. 829.

46. Quoted in Massie, *Land of the Firebird,* p. 321.

47. Quoted in Massie, *Land of the Firebird,* p. 323.

CHAPTER 6: RUSSIA IN THE WORLD COMMUNITY

48. "Under-Monitored Nuclear Materials Pose Threat," *Dow Jones Business News,* March 13, 1997. Downloaded from the Publications Library of The Wall Street Journal Interactive edition at www.wsj.com.

49. Michael R. Gordon, "Russia Thwarting U.S. Bid to Remove Nuclear Cache," *New York Times,* January 5, 1997, p. A1.

50. "Ukraine, Azerbaijan Unhappy with Russia Role in CIS," *Dow Jones Business News,* March 25, 1997. Downloaded from the Publications Library of The Wall Street Journal Interactive edition at www.wsj.com.

51. Sergei Grigoriev, "Rhetoric and Reality: Post-Soviet Policy in the Near Abroad," *Harvard International Review,* Winter 1996–97, p. 21.

52. Quoted in Grigoriev, "Rhetoric and Reality," p. 22.

53. David E. Mark, "Eurasia Letter: Russia and the New Transcaucasus," *Foreign Policy,* Winter 1996, p. 141.

54. Sherman Garnett, "Slow Dance: The Evolution of Sino-Russian Relations," *Harvard International Review,* Winter 1996–97, p. 31.

55. Sherman Garnett, "Slow Dance," p. 66.

56. "Russia, Iraq Sign Huge Oil Deal," *United Press International,* March 21, 1997. Downloaded from www.yahoo.com/headlines/.

57. Kenneth R. Timmerman, "And Now for the Real Arms Race," *Wall Street Journal Interactive Edition,* March 24, 1997. Downloaded from the Publications Library of The Wall Street Journal Interactive edition at www.wsj.com.

SUGGESTIONS FOR FURTHER READING

James H. Billington, *The Icon and the Axe*. New York: Knopf, 1966. The cultural development of the Russians from 1300 to the twentieth century.

Anton Chekhov, *The Island: A Journey to Sakhalin*. New York: Washington Square Press, 1967. The writer's account of his 1890 journey to the tsar's notorious penal colonies.

Prince George Galitzine, *Imperial Splendor: Palaces and Monasteries of Old Russia*. New York: Viking, 1992. A beautiful picture book of palaces and monasteries.

John Lawrence, *A History of Russia*. New York: Penguin Books, 1993. An easy-to-read retelling of Russia's history, available in paperback.

Robert K. Massie, *Peter the Great*. New York: Knopf, 1981. An engrossing biography. Also see *Nicholas and Alexandra* (1967) and *The Romanovs: The Final Chapter* (1995) by the same author.

Natalia Pushkareva, *Women in Russian History*. Armonk, NY: M. E. Sharpe, 1997. An important survey of this neglected topic.

David Remnick, *Resurrection: The Struggle for a New Russia*. New York: Random House, 1997. A lively portrait of the new Russian state.

David Satter, *Age of Delirium: The Decline and Fall of the Soviet Union*. New York: Knopf, 1996. A vivid account of the events leading to the Soviet collapse.

Theodore Von Laue and Angela Von Laue, *Faces of a Nation: The Rise and Fall of the Soviet Union, 1917–1991*. Golden, CO: Fulcrum, 1996. Contains outstanding photographs by Dmitri Baltermants.

WORKS CONSULTED

BOOKS

Robert Andrews, ed., *The Columbia Dictionary of Quotations.* New York: Columbia University Press, 1993. This standard reference work for students, writers, and scholars contains a wide variety of quotations organized by key word.

Paul Avrich, *Russian Rebels: 1600–1800.* New York: Schocken Books, 1972. A lively recounting of important rebellions which will help readers understand later revolutionary developments.

William Rose Benét, ed., *The Reader's Encyclopedia.* New York: Thomas Y. Crowell, 1965. This source provides annotations on authors, titles, and characters of major works of poetry and prose.

Jerome Blum, *Lord and Peasant in Russia.* Princeton, NJ: Princeton University Press, 1961. A classic in social history, this great resource illuminates the basic nature of Russian society.

Moshe Brawer, *Atlas of Russia and the Independent Republics.* New York: Simon and Schuster, 1994. A valuable and detailed description of natural features, this atlas offers information not found elsewhere.

Archie Brown, ed., *The Cambridge Encyclopedia of Russia and the Former Soviet Union.* Cambridge, England: Cambridge University Press, 1994. The most complete reference book available, this volume covers history and society up to the early 1990s.

John Channon with Robert Hudson, *The Penguin Historical Atlas of Russia.* New York: Penguin Books, 1995. This excellent summary helps readers visualize and conceptualize changes on the Eurasian continent.

Jesse D. Clarkson, *A History of Russia.* New York: Random House, 1961. Written with depth and understanding, this is a dependable history.

Zita Dabars, *The Russian Way: Aspects of Behavior, Attitudes, and Customs of the Russians.* Lincolnwood, IL: Passport Books, 1995. This book adds significant information about the everyday life of Russians.

Basil Dmytryshyn, ed., *Medieval Russia: A Source Book, 900–1700.* New York: Holt, Rinehart and Winston, 1967. Useful compilation of historic documents.

Martin Gilbert, *Imperial Russian History Atlas.* New York: Oxford Universiy Press, 1993. An essential resource to trace the expansion of Russia from a tiny principality to an empire, this should be read alongside any other history book.

Minton F. Goldman, *Russia, the Eurasian Republics, and Central/Eastern Europe.* Guilford, NC: Dushkin, 1994. This is a good source for contemporary documents on Russia and its neighbors.

Rhoda Hoff, *Russia: Adventures in Eyewitness History.* New York: Henry Z. Walck, 1964. A useful collection of historic documents and eyewitness accounts.

Paul Johnson, *Modern Times: The World from the Twenties to the Eighties.* New York: Harper & Row, 1983. A not-to-be-missed social, economic, and historical overview.

Lionel Kochan and Richard Abraham, *The Making of Modern Russia.* London: Penguin Books, 1988. A good basic history, available in paperback.

Richard Layard and John Parker, *The Coming Russian Boom.* New York: Free Press, 1996. Up-to-date information on Russia's economy.

Richard Leonard, *A History of Russian Music.* New York: Macmillan, 1957. Still valuable, although a more recent edition would be welcome.

Suzanne Massie, *Land of the Firebird: The Beauty of Old Russia.* New York: Simon and Schuster, 1980. This well-written account of the development of the arts remains a standard text.

Paul Miliukov, *History of Russia.* New York: Funk & Wagnalls, 1968. This work is important for its Russian point of view.

Peter Neville, *A Traveller's History of Russia and the USSR.* New York: Interlink Books, 1994. A keenly observed and well-written narrative of Russia's history, including a historical gazetteer.

R. R. Palmer and Joel Colton, *A History of the Modern World Since 1815.* New York: McGraw-Hill, 1995. A coherent, useful overview, with an especially valuable bibliography.

Richard Pipes, *A Concise History of the Russian Revolution.* New York: Knopf, 1995. An exceptionally well written, thorough, and dependable resource. Other books on Russian history by the same author are well worth reading.

Richard Pipes, ed., *The Unknown Lenin.* New Haven, CT: Yale University Press, 1996. Fascinating, previously unpublished material.

Thomas Riha, ed., *Readings in Russian Civilization.* Chicago: University of Chicago Press, 1969. An anthology of important historic documents.

Ivar Spector, ed., *Readings in Russian History and Culture.* Boston: Allyn and Bacon, 1965. A collection of historic documents.

Tacitus, *Germania.* Cambridge, MA: Harvard University Press, 1970. This fascinating history should be read in its entirety.

George Vernadsky, *Ancient Russia.* New Haven, CT: Yale University Press, 1959. A still indispensable classic, with fascinating detail. Followed by three other volumes, several updates, and abridgments.

George Vernadsky, ed., *A Source Book for Russian History from Early Times to 1917.* 3 vols. New Haven, CT: Yale University Press, 1972. A companion to Vernadsky's great histories.

Arthur Voyce, *Moscow and the Roots of Russian Culture.* Norman: University of Oklahoma Press, 1964. An insightful discussion of the cultural and artistic traditions of Russia's greatest city.

Warren Walsh, ed., *Readings in Russian History from Ancient Times to the Post-Stalin Era.* 2 vols. Syracuse, NY: Syracuse University Press, 1963. An indispensable collection of readings not found elsewhere.

PERIODICALS

Vanora Bennet, "Russia: Crime Pays, the State Doesn't," *Los Angeles Times,* November 28, 1996, home edition.

Sherman Garnett, "Slow Dance: The Evolution of Sino-Russian Relations," *Harvard International Review,* Winter 1996–97.

"Godfather of the Kremlin: Russian Crime Boss Boris Berezovsky," *Forbes,* December 30, 1996.

Michael R. Gordon, "Russia Thwarting U.S. Bid to Remove a Nuclear Cache," *New York Times,* January 5, 1997.

Sergei Grigoriev, "Rhetoric and Reality: Post-Soviet Policy in the Near Abroad," *Harvard International Review,* Winter 1996–1997.

Olga Listosova, "The Holy Image Makers," *Russian Life,* December 1996.

David E. Mark, "Eurasia Letter: Russia and the New Transcaucasus," *Foreign Policy,* Winter 1996.

"Russia, Iraq Sign Huge Oil Deal," *United Press International,* March 21, 1997.

Avraham Shama, "Inside Russia's True Economy," *Foreign Policy,* Summer 1996.

"Solzhenitsyn: Russia Joining Third World," *Reuters Limited,* March 23, 1997.

Alessandra Stanley, "From Russia, with Songs of Days Long Gone, to the U.S.," *New York Times,* April 1, 1997.

"Still Going for Gold," *Russian Life,* July 1996.

"That Charging Bear Is a Russian Bull (Market)," *Baron's,* March 10, 1997.

Kenneth R. Timmerman, "And Now for the Real Arms Race," *Wall Street Journal Interactive Edition,* March 24, 1997.

"Ukraine, Azerbaijan Unhappy with Russia Role in CIS," *Dow Jones Business News,* March 25, 1997.

"Under-Monitored Nuclear Materials Pose Threat," *Dow Jones Business News,* March 13, 1997.

INDEX

PICTURE CREDITS

ABOUT THE AUTHOR

Kim Brown Fader was educated at Brown University in Providence, Rhode Island, and City College in New York City, where she studied history, English, and creative writing. She has written for a number of national publications, including *Glamour, Parenting, Seventeen, Parents,* and *USA Today.* This is her first book for Lucent Books.